Microsoft® Office Excel® 2007

Level 1 (Second Edition)

Microsoft® Office Excel® 2007: Level 1 (Second Edition)

Part Number: 084890
Course Edition: 1.10

NOTICES

What is the Microsoft Business Certification Program?

The Microsoft Business Certification Program enables candidates to show that they have something exceptional to offer – proven expertise in Microsoft Office programs. The two certification tracks allow candidates to choose how they want to exhibit their skills, either through validating skills within a specific Microsoft product or taking their knowledge to the next level and combining Microsoft programs to show that they can apply multiple skill sets to complete more complex office tasks. Recognized by businesses and schools around the world, over 3 million certifications have been obtained in over 100 different countries. The Microsoft Business Certification Program is the only Microsoft-approved certification program of its kind.

What is the Microsoft Certified Application Specialist Certification?

Your comments are important to us. Please contact us at Element K Press LLC, 1-800-478-7788, 500 Canal View Boulevard, Rochester, NY 14623, Attention: Product Planning, or through our Web site at **http://support.elementkcourseware.com.**

The Microsoft Certified Application Specialist Certification exams focus on validating specific skill sets within each of the Microsoft® Office system programs. The candidate can choose which exam(s) they want to take according to which skills they want to validate. The available Application Specialist exams include:

- Using Microsoft®Windows Vista™
- Using Microsoft® Office Word 2007
- Using Microsoft® Office Excel® 2007
- Using Microsoft® Office PowerPoint® 2007
- Using Microsoft® Office Access 2007
- Using Microsoft® Office Outlook® 2007

What is the Microsoft Certified Application Professional Certification?

The Microsoft Certified Application Professional Certification exams focus on a candidate's ability to use the 2007 Microsoft® Office system to accomplish industry-agnostic functions, for example Budget Analysis and Forecasting, or Content Management and Collaboration. The available Application Professional exams currently include:

- Organizational Support
- Creating and Managing Presentations
- Content Management and Collaboration
- Budget Analysis and Forecasting

What do the Microsoft Business Certification Vendor of Approved Courseware logos represent?

The logos validate that the courseware has been approved by the Microsoft® Business Certification Vendor program and that these courses cover objectives that will be included in the relevant exam. It also means that after utilizing this courseware, you may be prepared to pass the exams required to become a Microsoft Certified Application Specialist or Microsoft Certified Application Professional.

For more information:

To learn more about Microsoft Certified Application Specialist or Professional exams, visit **www.microsoft.com/learning/msbc**.

To learn about other Microsoft Certified Application Specialist approved courseware from Element K, visit **www.elementkcourseware.com**.

* The availability of Microsoft Certified Application exams varies by Microsoft Office program, program version and language. Visit **www.microsoft.com/learning** for exam availability.

Microsoft, the Office Logo, Outlook, and PowerPoint are either registered trademarks or trademarks of Microsoft Corporation in the United States and/or other countries. The Microsoft Certified Application Specialist and Microsoft Certified Application Professional Logos are used under license from Microsoft Corporation.

Microsoft® Office Excel® 2007: Level 1 (Second Edition)

About This Course

You have basic computer skills such as using a mouse, navigating through windows, and surfing the Internet. You have also used paper-based systems to store data that you run calculations on. You now want to migrate that data to an electronic format.

When you use a paper-based method to store data, you need to erase the totals row every time you add a new row of data. The totals row has be to re-written after manually adding the newly added data with the previous total. This is time consuming and can cause data loss. In an electronic spreadsheet, you can simply insert a new row and add the new data. The totals row could be set to update whenever the data changes.

Storing data electronically is more efficient because it allows you to quickly update existing data, run reports on the data, calculate totals, and chart, sort, and filter your data.

This course can also benefit you if you are preparing to take the Microsoft Certified Application Specialist exam for Microsoft® Excel® 2007. Please refer to the CD-ROM that came with this course for a document that maps exam objectives to the content in the Microsoft Office Excel Courseware series. To access the mapping document, insert the CD-ROM into your CD-ROM drive and at the root of the ROM, double-click ExamMapping.doc to open the mapping document. In addition to the mapping document, two assessment files per course can be found on the CD-ROM to check your knowledge. To access the assessments, at the root of the course part number folder, double-click 084890s3.doc to view the assessments without the answers marked, or double-click 084890ie.doc to view the assessments with the answers marked.

f your book did not come with a CD, please go to http://www.elementk.com/courseware-file-downloads to download the data files.

Course Description

Target Student

This course is designed for people preparing for certification as a Microsoft Certified Application Specialist in Excel, who already have knowledge of Microsoft® Office, Windows® 2000 (or above), and who desire to gain the skills necessary to create, edit, format, and print basic Microsoft Office Excel 2007 worksheets.

Course Prerequisites

Students should be familiar with using personal computers and have used a mouse and keyboard. You should be comfortable in the Windows environment and be able to use Windows to manage information on your computer. Specifically, you should be able to launch and close programs; navigate to information stored on the computer; and manage files and folders. Students should have completed the following courses or possess equivalent knowledge before starting with this course:

■   *Windows XP Professional: Level 1*

■   *Windows XP Professional: Level 2*

■   *Windows XP: Introduction*

■   *Windows 2000: Introduction*

How to Use This Book

As a Learning Guide

Each lesson covers one broad topic or set of related topics. Lessons are arranged in order of increasing proficiency with *Excel 2007*; skills you acquire in one lesson are used and developed in subsequent lessons. For this reason, you should work through the lessons in sequence.

We organized each lesson into results-oriented topics. Topics include all the relevant and supporting information you need to master *Excel 2007*, and activities allow you to apply this information to practical hands-on examples.

You get to try out each new skill on a specially prepared sample file. This saves you typing time and allows you to concentrate on the skill at hand. Through the use of sample files, hands-on activities, illustrations that give you feedback at crucial steps, and supporting background information, this book provides you with the foundation and structure to learn *Excel 2007* quickly and easily.

As a Review Tool

Any method of instruction is only as effective as the time and effort you are willing to invest in it. In addition, some of the information that you learn in class may not be important to you immediately, but it may become important later on. For this reason, we encourage you to spend some time reviewing the topics and activities after the course. For additional challenge when reviewing activities, try the "What You Do" column before looking at the "How You Do It" column.

As a Reference

The organization and layout of the book make it easy to use as a learning tool and as an after-class reference. You can use this book as a first source for definitions of terms, background information on given topics, and summaries of procedures.

Course Icons

Icon	Description
	A **Caution Note** makes students aware of potential negative consequences of an action, setting, or decision that are not easily known.
	Display Slide provides a prompt to the instructor to display a specific slide. Display Slides are included in the Instructor Guide only.
	An **Instructor Note** is a comment to the instructor regarding delivery, class-room strategy, classroom tools, exceptions, and other special considerations. Instructor Notes are included in the Instructor Guide only.
	Notes Page indicates a page that has been left intentionally blank for students to write on.
	A **Student Note** provides additional information, guidance, or hints about a topic or task.
	A **Version Note** indicates information necessary for a specific version of software.

Certification

This course is designed to help you prepare for the following certification.

Certification Path: Microsoft Certified Application Specialist – Excel® 2007

This course is one of a series of Element K courseware titles that addresses Microsoft Certified Application Specialist (Microsoft Business Certification) skill sets. The Microsoft Certified Application Specialist program is for individuals who use Microsoft's business desktop software and who seek recognition for their expertise with specific Microsoft products. Certification candidates must pass one or more proficiency exams in order to earn Microsoft Certified Application Specialist certification.

Course Objectives

In this course, you will create and edit basic Microsoft® Office Excel® 2007 worksheets and workbooks.

You will:

- explore the Microsoft® Office Excel® 2007 environment and create a basic worksheet.
- perform calculations.
- modify a worksheet.
- format a worksheet.
- print workbook contents.
- manage large workbooks.

Course Requirements

Hardware

For this course, you will need one computer for each student and one for the instructor. Each computer will need the following minimum hardware components:

- A 1 GHz Pentium-class processor or faster.
- A minimum of 256 MB of RAM. 512 MB of RAM is recommended.
- A 10 GB hard disk or larger. You should have at least 1 GB of free hard disk space available for the Office installation.
- A CD-ROM drive.
- A keyboard and mouse or other pointing device.
- A 1024 x 768 resolution monitor is recommended.
- Network cards and cabling for local network access.
- Internet access (contact your local network administrator).
- A printer (optional) or an installed printer driver.
- A projection system to display the instructor's computer screen.

Software

- Microsoft Office Professional Edition 2007
- Microsoft Office Suite Service Pack 1
- Windows XP Professional with Service Pack 2

This course was developed using the Windows XP operating system; however, the manufacturer's documentation states that it will also run on Vista. If you use Vista, you might notice some slight differences when keying the course.

Class Setup

Initial class setup

For initial class setup:

1. Install Windows XP Professional on an empty partition.

   ■ Leave the Administrator password blank.

   ■ For all other installation parameters, use values that are appropriate for your environ-ment (see your local network administrator for details).

2. On Windows XP Professional, disable the Welcome screen. (This step ensures that stu-dents will be able to log on as the Administrator user regardless of what other user accounts exist on the computer.)

   a. Click Start and choose Control Panel→User Accounts.

   b. Click Change The Way Users Log On And Off.

   c. Uncheck Use Welcome Screen.

   d. Click Apply Options.

3. On Windows XP Professional, install Service Pack 2. Use the Service Pack installation defaults.

4. On the computer, install a printer driver (a physical print device is optional). Click Start and choose Printers And Faxes. Under Printer Tasks, click Add A Printer and follow the prompts.

   If you do not have a physical printer installed, right-click the printer and choose Pause Printing to prevent any print error messages.

5. Run the Internet Connection Wizard to set up the Internet connection as appropriate for your environment if you did not do so during installation.

6. Display known file type extensions.

   a. Open Windows Explorer (right-click Start and then select Explore).

   b. Choose Tools→Folder Options.

   c. On the View tab, in the Advanced Settings list box, uncheck Hide Extensions For Known File Types.

   d. Click Apply, and then click OK.

   e. Close Windows Explorer.

7. Log on to the computer as the Administrator user if you have not already done so.

8. Perform a Complete installation of Microsoft Office Professional 2007.

9. In the User Name dialog box, click OK to accept the default user name and initials.

10. In the Microsoft Office 2007 Activation Wizard dialog box, click Next to activate the Office 2007 application.

11. When the activation of Microsoft Office 2007 is complete, click Close to close the Microsoft Office 2007 Activation Wizard dialog box.

12. In the User Name dialog box, click OK.

13. In the Welcome To Microsoft 2007! dialog box, click Finish. You must have an active Internet connection in order to complete this step. Here, you select the Download And Install Updates From Microsoft Update When Available (Recommended) option, so that whenever there is a new update, it gets automatically installed in your system.

14. After the Microsoft Update runs, in the Microsoft Office dialog box, click OK.

If your book did not come with a CD, please go to **http:// www.elementk.com/ courseware-file-downloads** to download the data files.

15. On the course CD-ROM, open the 084_890 folder. Then, open the Data folder. Run the 084890dd.exe self-extracting file located in it. This will install a folder named 084890Data on your C drive. This folder contains all the data files that you will use to complete this course.

    Within each lesson folder, you may find a Solution folder. This folder contains solution files for the lesson's activities and lesson lab, which can be used by students to check their end results.

16. If necessary, minimize the Language Bar.

Customize the Windows Desktop

Customize the Windows desktop to display the My Computer and My Network Places icon on the student and instructor systems:

1. Right-click the Desktop and choose Properties.
2. Select the Desktop tab.
3. Click Customize Desktop.
4. In the Desktop Items dialog box, check My Computer and My Network Places.
5. Click OK and click Apply.
6. Close the Display Properties dialog box.

Before Every Class

1. Log on to the computer as the Administrator user.
2. Delete any existing data files from the C:\084890Data folder.
3. Extract a fresh copy of the course data files from the CD-ROM provided with the course manual.

List of Additional Files

Printed with each activity is a list of files students open to complete that activity. Many activities also require additional files that students do not open, but are needed to support the file(s) students are working with. These supporting files are included with the student data files on the course CD-ROM or data disk. Do not delete these files.

1 | Creating a Basic Worksheet

Lesson Time: 1 hour(s), 10 minutes

Lesson Objectives:

In this lesson, you will explore the Microsoft® Office Excel® 2007 environment and create a basic worksheet.

You will:

- Identify the components of the Excel user interface, including the Ribbon.
- Navigate and select data in Excel.
- Obtain help to find relevant information needed to perform a task in Excel.
- Enter data and save a worksheet.
- Customize the Quick Access toolbar.

Introduction

You have heard that Microsoft® Office Excel® 2007 can help you store and manage alphanumeric data, and you would like to use the application, but you are not familiar with its environment. In this lesson, you will explore the Excel environment to familiarize yourself with some of its basic concepts.

Imagine using a computer without having a basic understanding of its components and how it operates. Similarly, using a software application, such as Excel, without understanding its basic components would be difficult. Exploring the Excel environment will introduce you to some of its basic tools and functions, which will help you get started with Excel.

TOPIC A

Explore the User Interface and the Ribbon

You are not familiar with Excel and would like to use the application to store and manipulate data. Before working with the application, you need to familiarize yourself with its basic interface components. In this topic, you will explore the user interface of Excel.

Wouldn't it be easier for you to perform in your new job if you received an overview of how to work in your new environment? Similarly, exploring Excel's user interface will help you to familiarize yourself with some of its basic functions, which, in turn, will help you work on the application effectively.

Spreadsheets

Definition:

A *spreadsheet* is a paper or an electronic document that stores various types of data, such as numbers, text, and non-alphanumeric symbols, in a tabular format. A spreadsheet consists of vertical columns and horizontal rows that intersect to form cells. The cells store the data entered into a spreadsheet. Users can then manipulate the data in the cells or run calculations on the data. Spreadsheets differ from one another based on their associated business needs and data requirements.

Example:

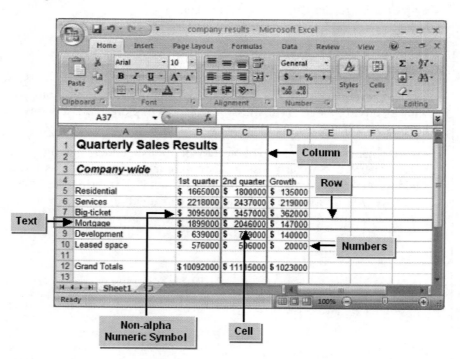

Figure 1-1: A spreadsheet.

Microsoft Office Excel 2007

Excel 2007 is an application in the Microsoft Office suite that can be used to create, revise, and save data in a spreadsheet format. It is used to perform calculations using formulas and functions. The Excel application can also be used to analyze, share, and manage information using charts and tables.

The Excel Application Window

When you launch Excel, two windows are displayed, one within the other. The outer window is the main *application window*, and the inner window is the *workbook window*. The application window usually fills the entire screen and provides a place for you to interact with Excel. The workbook window appears within the application window and is used for entering data.

The Excel application window has various advanced components.

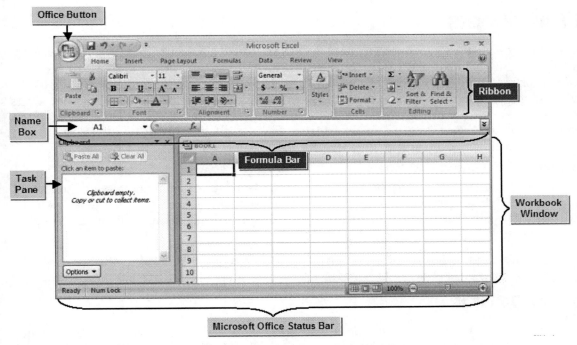

Figure 1-2: The Excel application window has various components.

Window Element	Description
The Office button	A standard button that displays a menu containing various functions to open, save, print, and close an Excel file.
The Quick Access toolbar	A toolbar that provides easy access to frequently used commands in the application.
The Ribbon	A panel that houses the command buttons and icons, organized into a set of tabs.

Window Element	Description
Formula Bar	A bar that contains the Name Box, the Formula Box, and the Insert Function button. The Name Box displays the name of the currently selected cell in a spreadsheet. The Formula Box displays the contents of the currently selected cell in a spreadsheet and allows you to type the formula or function required. The Insert Function button displays the options to insert a function.
Task pane	A pane that appears on an as needed basis with several options for a particular command selected on the Ribbon. You can move and resize the task pane.
The Microsoft Office Status Bar	A window element that contains features such as the dynamic zoom slider and the customizable status display.

Worksheets

A *worksheet* is a spreadsheet used to store data in the Excel application. An Excel worksheet contains 16,384 columns and 1,048,576 rows that intersect to form grids. The entire Excel worksheet is comprised of gridlines that form rectangles called cells. One cell is always selected and is called the *active cell*. By default, Excel designates column headings with letters running across the top of the worksheet and row headings with numbers running down the left border of the worksheet. You can insert or delete rows or columns in an Excel worksheet. An Excel worksheet can contain text, numbers, formulas, charts, or tables.

Worksheet Columns and Rows

Column headings in Excel worksheets begin with the letter A and continue through the letter Z. After the 26th column (column Z), headings become double letters, from AA to AZ. After AZ, the letter pairs start again with columns BA through BZ, and so on, until all 16,384 columns have alphabetical headings, ending at XFD.

Row headings begin with the number 1 and continue through the number 1,048,576.

Workbooks

A *workbook* is an Excel file that acts as a repository for related Excel worksheets. By default, an Excel workbook contains three worksheets named Sheet1, Sheet2, and Sheet3. The worksheet names appear on tabs at the bottom of the workbook. You can rename the worksheet tabs, and you can also add or remove worksheets from an Excel workbook.

An Excel workbook contains various elements.

Workbook Element	Description
Title bar	Appears above the Ribbon and center-aligns the name of the workbook. The Quick Access toolbar is integrated into the title bar.
Home Tab bar	Appears at the bottom of the workbook and contains the Tab scrolling buttons, the worksheet tabs, and the Insert Worksheet button. It also contains the integrated horizontal scroll bar.
Worksheet tab	Appears at the bottom of the workbook on the Home Tab bar, and allows you to move from one worksheet to another.

Workbook Element	Description
Tab scrolling button	Appears at the left of the sheet tabs on the Home Tab bar and allows you to scroll the display of the worksheet tabs one at a time, or display the first or last grouping of sheet tabs within a workbook.
Insert Worksheet button	Appears to the left of the worksheet tabs on the Home Tab bar, and is used to add new worksheets.

The Office button

The *Office button* is a standard button located at the top-left corner of the Excel window that contains commands to open, save, send, print, close, prepare, and publish worksheets. Each menu contains various submenu options. The Office button also provides options to customize the Excel environment. The menu retains a list of recently used worksheets, enabling you to access them quickly.

The Quick Access Toolbar

The *Quick Access toolbar* is located above the Ribbon and is displayed as an integrated component of the title bar to provide convenient access to frequently used commands in the application. By default, the toolbar holds the Save, Undo, and Redo commands in the form of buttons. You can customize the Quick Access toolbar to include additional commands that you frequently use. However, when additional commands are added, the title bar space is reduced, diminishing the title display of the open document. You can avoid this inconvenience by relocating the Quick Access toolbar below the Ribbon using options in the Customize Quick Access Toolbar drop-down list.

Figure 1-3: The Quick Access toolbar.

The Microsoft Office Status Bar

The *Microsoft Office Status Bar* is located at the bottom of the Excel window. It indicates whether options, such as cell mode, end mode, page number, and macros, are turned on or off. It is a component that has features for enriching the worksheet-authoring experience in Excel 2007. It contains features such as the dynamic zoom slider and the customizable status display.

The Microsoft Office Status Bar contains several components.

Feature	Description
Status display	Contains several additional options that can be calculated and displayed. The display allows the output of multiple values and specifies the action being performed on the worksheet. For instance, data being entered, count, average, and sum of numbers.
View buttons	Provide the options to display the worksheet in any of the three types of views that have been provided by default: Normal, Page Layout, and Page Break.
Zoom Out button	Allows you to view contents in a worksheet in a smaller size.
Zoom slider	Allows you to magnify or minimize the worksheet instantaneously to any desired size.
Zoom In button	Allows you to have an enlarged view of contents in a worksheet.
Zoom button	Allows you to select or set the zoom percentage in the Zoom dialog box.

The Ribbon

The *Ribbon* is a unique interface component that comprises several task-specific commands that are grouped together under different command tabs. It is designed to be the primary location for accessing commands.

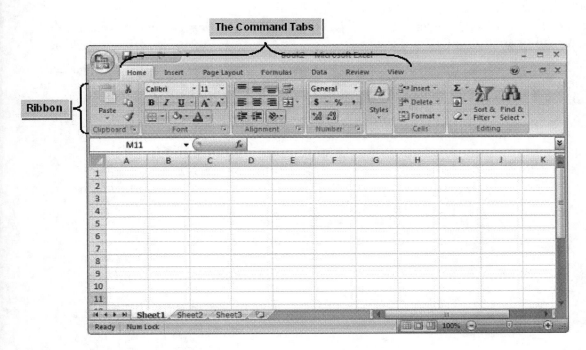

Figure 1-4: *The Ribbon in Excel.*

Command Tabs

The following table lists the command tabs on the Ribbon in Excel.

Command Tab	Description
Home	Used for performing clipboard operations and basic text and cell formatting.
Insert	Used for inserting tables, charts, illustrations, text, and links.
Page Layout	Used for specifying page settings, layout, orientation, margins and other related options.
Formulas	Used for creating formulas with built-in functions that are categorized by the type of calculations you need to perform.
Data	Used to establish connections with external data sources and import data for use within Excel worksheets.
Review	Used during the review of Excel worksheets and provides tools such as spell checker, thesaurus, and translator.
View	Used to hide or display gridlines in a worksheet, and provides options to control the display of the worksheet and the application window.

Contextual Tabs

Contextual tabs are command tabs that appear on the Ribbon only when you select specific objects on the worksheet such as a chart, table, drawing, text box, or WordArt. These tabs are displayed in addition to the existing command tabs. Since these tabs are context based, the scope of their commands and tools is restricted to only the objects in which they are specialized.

ScreenTips

A ScreenTip is descriptive text that is displayed when you position the mouse pointer on a command or control in the interface.

An Enhanced ScreenTip uses a larger block of descriptive text than a ScreenTip. Enhanced ScreenTips can contain a link to a Help topic. Most of the buttons and features in Excel have associated Enhanced ScreenTips.

ACTIVITY 1-1

Exploring the User Interface

Scenario:
You need to enter your company's employee information into an Excel worksheet. You are not familiar with the application and would like to familiarize yourself with its interface elements before starting to work in it.

What You Do	How You Do It
1. **Explore the Office button.**	a. **Choose Start→All Programs→Microsoft Office→Microsoft Office Excel 2007** to open the Microsoft Office Excel 2007 application.
	b. In the top-left corner of the Microsoft Excel window, **click the Office button.**
	c. There are various options on the Office button menu. **Place the mouse pointer over the Save As option** to view the submenu options.
	d. **Click outside the Office button menu** to close it.

2. **Explore the Ribbon.**

    a. On the Ribbon, **select the Page Layout tab.**

    b. Notice that the Page Layout tab consists of the Themes, Page Setup, Scale To Fit, Sheet Options, and Arrange groups.

    c. In the Page Setup group, **place the mouse pointer over the Margins button** to view its screentip.

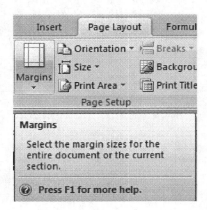

    d. **Select each of the other tabs in the Ribbon** to view the commands and the groups they contain.

3. **Explore the Quick Access toolbar.**

    a. On the Quick Access toolbar, **place the mouse pointer over each button** to view its screentip.

    b. **Click the Customize Quick Access Toolbar drop-down arrow** to view the options.

    c. **Press Esc.**

4. **Explore the Microsoft Office Status Bar.**

a. On the Microsoft Office Status Bar, **place the mouse pointer over each of the view buttons to the left of the Zoom slider** to view its description.

b. On the Zoom slider, **click the Zoom In button.**

c. Notice that the zoom percentage has increased to 110%.

d. **Click the Zoom Out button.** ⊖

e. Notice that the zoom percentage has reverted to 100%.

TOPIC B
Navigate and Select in Excel

You familiarized yourself with the various interface components of the Excel environment. Now, you want to start working in the Excel environment. In order to view or modify data in Excel, you need to know how to navigate through the worksheet and select cells. In this topic, you will navigate through an Excel worksheet and select a range of cells.

Imagine you've just moved to a new city to start a new job. You've only been in the new place for about a week and haven't really had the time to take a closer look around the city. You've set aside time in the upcoming weekend to drive around the city and begin familiarizing yourself with some of the landmarks. Learning the basics of navigating in Excel is much like this: you know how to drive, but you don't know the terrain yet. By navigating around Excel, you begin to understand its terrain, thus making it easier for you to work with data in a worksheet.

The Open Dialog Box

The Open command, from the Office button menu, displays the Open dialog box. The Open dialog box has options to search for existing files to be opened. In the Open dialog box, the Look In drop-down list allows you to select the directory and navigate to the desired file. You can then open the selected file by double-clicking it. The Files Of Type drop-down list provides options to select the format in which the file needs to be opened. The Open button in the Open dialog box lists various options as to how the file should be opened. You can open the original file, open a copy of the file, or open the file as read-only.

 If you want to open a recently used file, you can access it from the Office button menu, where the recently opened documents are listed.

Mouse Navigation Options

By using the mouse to work with the horizontal and vertical scroll bars, you can navigate to a specific cell, range of cells, or to the end of ranges.

Navigation	Action
To move the worksheet display up or down one row per click	Click a vertical scroll arrow.
To move the worksheet display left or right one column per click	Click a horizontal scroll arrow.
To continuously move the worksheet display horizontally or vertically	Continuously click the horizontal or vertical scroll arrows.
To move the worksheet display one screen at a time	Click between the scroll box and the scroll arrow of either the horizontal or vertical scroll bar.

Navigation	Action
To move rapidly, either vertically or horizontally, through the worksheet area	Drag the scroll boxes.
To move to the cell specified in the cell reference	Click in the Name Box, type the cell reference, and press Enter.

Keyboard Navigation Options

You can also use the keyboard to navigate to a specific cell, range of cells, or to the end of ranges in a worksheet.

To Move the Active Cell	Do This
One cell at a time to the left, right, up, or down	Press the corresponding arrow keys.
To column A of the current row	Press Home.
Down or up by one screen's worth of rows	Press Page Down or Page Up.
To the right, one cell at a time	Press Tab.
To the left, one cell at a time	Press Shift+Tab.
To cell A1 in the active worksheet	Press Ctrl+Home.
One screen to the left or right	Press Alt+Page Up to go left. Press Alt+Page Down to go right.

Selection Options

There are many ways to select cells or groups of cells in a worksheet.

Selection	Action
A single cell	Click the cell.
The contents of a cell	Double-click the cell to place the insertion point inside the cell, and then double-click again to select the contents of the cell. You can also select the cell, and then select the contents of the formula text box.
A contiguous range of cells	A *contiguous* range consists of cells that are all adjacent. Select the first cell in the contiguous range, press and hold Shift, navigate to the last cell in the range, and then click the last cell to select the full range. You can also click and drag from the first cell to the last cell to select the range.
A noncontiguous range of cells	A *noncontiguous* range consists of cells that are not adjacent. Select the first cell in the first range, press and hold Ctrl, navigate to the next cell in the range, and click the next cell. You can combine the Shift+click and Ctrl+click methods if preferred.
An entire worksheet	Click the Select All button immediately below the Name Box. You can also press Ctrl+A.

ACTIVITY 1-2
Navigating and Selecting in Excel

Data Files:

Employee Info.xlsx

Before You Begin:

Microsoft Office Excel 2007 is open.

Scenario:

You are the newly appointed HR executive of a company. You would like to locate an employee's department. You decide to view the company's employee information worksheet.

What You Do	How You Do It
1. **Open the Employee Info file.**	a. In the Excel window, **click the Office button and choose Open.**
	b. In the Open dialog box, **navigate to the C:\084890Data\Creating a Basic Worksheet folder.**
	c. **Select the Employee Info.xlsx file and click Open.**
2. **View the last employee.**	a. Using the vertical scroll bar, **scroll down** to view the last row.
	b. **Click row heading 98** to select the last employee.
3. **View the contents of cell G50.**	a. On the Formula Bar, **click in the Name Box.**
	b. **Type *G50* and press Enter** to view the contents of cell G50.

G50					fx	12/30/1988	
	A	B	C	D	E	F	G
50	46 Lance	Davies	GBC64	Connecticut	Development		30-Dec-1988
51	47 Anne	Davidson	CC23	New Hampsh	Development		6-Apr-1986

4.	**Locate the Total Hours cell.**	a.	On the keyboard, **press Ctrl+Home** to view cell A1.
		b.	Using the horizontal scroll bar, **scroll to the right** to view the total hours in cells P4 and P5.

5.	**Select a range of cells.**	a.	**Click cell B2.**
		b.	**Hold down Shift and click cell D41.**

6.	**Select an entire worksheet.**	a.	In the top-left corner of the worksheet, below the Name Box, **click the Select All button** to select the entire worksheet.
		b.	**Click the Office button and choose Close.**
		c.	If necessary, in the Microsoft Office Excel message box, **click No** to close the workbook without saving it.

TOPIC C
Obtain Help

You have navigated through an Excel worksheet and explored various selection techniques. It should be reassuring to know that you don't have to remember everything. The Excel help is available to you at any time for the additional support when you need. In this topic, you will learn how to obtain help in Excel.

You are working on a workbook and find yourself constantly using the mouse to navigate between cells, but you prefer to use keyboard shortcuts as much as possible. With the Excel help system, you can find information on how to move through a worksheet using keyboard shortcuts. By accessing the Excel help feature, you can find relevant offline and online information needed to perform a task in Excel.

The Excel Help Window

You can use the Microsoft Office Excel Help button, on the top-right corner of the Excel application window, to access the *Excel Help window*. The Excel Help window has options that enable you to find answers to Excel-related questions, allowing you to search for information available both online and offline.

The Excel Help window has various elements.

Window Element	Description
Toolbar	Provides access to navigational, print, and format commands.
Type Words To Search For text box	Allows you to specify the query you are searching for.
Search drop-down list	Allows you to specify if the search has to be performed online or offline.
Browse Excel Help pane	Displays the various topic links available on Excel Help. You can navigate to a topic link by clicking it.

Areas of Search

The Search drop-down list helps to narrow the search results to a specific area. You can either use the Content From This Computer options to search for information from within the Excel application or select the Content From Office Online options to search the web.

Area of Search	Description
All Excel	Lists information on the query from the built-in Help and displays the Office online website, if required.
Excel Help	Lists information on the query from built-in Help as well as the Office online website, but does not take you to the Office online website.
Excel Templates	Lists sample templates that are available from the Office online website.

Area of Search	Description
Excel Training	Lists sample training information from the Office online website.
Developer Reference	Includes programming tasks, samples, and references to create customized solutions.

The Table Of Contents Pane

The Table Of Contents pane is displayed on the left of the Excel Help window and lists the help topic links for the various Excel features. You can click the topic links to display the sub-topic links. The sub-topic links display the relevant information in the right pane of the Excel Help window.

How to Obtain Help

Procedure Reference: Obtain Help

To find information in Excel Help:

1. Click the Help button in the Ribbon, or press F1, to open the Excel Help window.
2. If desired, click the Show Table Of Contents button to display the Table of Contents.
3. Click a link in the Table Of Contents pane or the Browse Excel Help list to view its details.
4. If desired, search for information.
    a. Select an option from the Search drop-down list to narrow the search to a particular area.
    b. In the Type Words To Search For text box, type a keyword.
    c. Click Search to display the search results.
5. Click the Close button to close the Excel Help window.

ACTIVITY 1-3

Obtaining Help

Before You Begin:

Your system should be connected to the Internet to access Office Online and Microsoft Office Excel 2007 is open.

Scenario:

You are new to the Excel 2007 interface; so you would like to get additional support and read more about an interface element. You also realize that knowing shortcut keys would be beneficial to your work in Excel. So you decide to search for information on shortcut methods used to perform an action.

What You Do	How You Do It
1. Search for information about the Ribbon.	a. On the Ribbon, **click the Microsoft Office Excel Help button.**
	b. In the Excel Help window, in the Type Words To Search For text box, **type *ribbon* and click Search.**
	c. In the displayed results, **click the Use The Ribbon link** to access the page that describes the Ribbon.
	d. View information about the Ribbon.

2. **Search for information about Excel shortcut keys.**

   a. In the Excel Help window, on the toolbar, **click the Show Table Of Contents button.**

   b. In the Table Of Contents pane, **click Accessibility.**

   c. Under Accessibility, in the displayed list of links, **scroll down and click Excel Shortcut And Function Keys.**

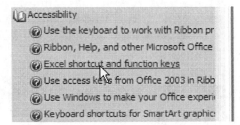

   d. In the right pane, **scroll down** to read the displayed information.

   e. In the top-right corner of the Excel Help window, **click the Close button** to close it.

TOPIC D
Enter Data and Save a Workbook

You have worked with an existing worksheet to navigate through the data, performed some various selection techniques and used Excel Help to locate some keyboard shortcuts and function keys. Now it is time to create a new workbook where you can add data and then save your work. In this topic, you will enter data and save your work.

In order to write a book, a writer has to fill the pages with words. Similarly, to create informative workbooks in Excel, you need to enter data into worksheets. There are many ways to organize your data, but a structure that column and row headings makes it much easier to identify the information.

The New Workbook Dialog Box

The New Workbook dialog box allows you to create either a blank workbook or a workbook based on a template that is available locally or that can be downloaded from Microsoft Office Online. You can access the New Workbook dialog box from the Office button menu. The left pane of the New Workbook dialog box contains the template categories. The subcategory and templates are listed in the middle pane of the New workbook window. The recently used templates are also listed in the middle pane. The templates are customizable and can suit specific requirements of businesses or individuals.

Data Types

Cells can contain text, numbers, or formulas. In a worksheet, text is used to organize and label the numerical information. By default, text is left aligned in the cell and numbers are right-aligned.

The Save and Save As Commands

Once the workbook has been created, you will need to save it so that you can access it again at a later time. Use the Save As command to save a file for the first time, and also to save an existing file with a new name, to change the file type, or to save it in a new directory. Use the Save command to save changes made to an existing workbook without changing its name, type, or directory.

 If you use the Save command when a workbook has not been previously saved, the Save As dialog box will automatically appear.

The Save As Dialog Box

In the Save As dialog box, from the Save In drop-down list, you can select the directory for the file. The default name of the file appears in the File Name text box. You can change the file name, if desired. From the Save As Type drop-down list, you can select the format in which to save the file.

Excel 2007 File Types

All Excel 2007 files use Extensible Markup Language (XML) as the basic file format. The Excel XML format is a compact, robust file format enabling easy integration of Excel files into other applications and platforms. Excel 2007 supports a number of other file types as well.

Other Excel File Formats

The following table lists some of the important file formats you can use in Excel 2007.

File Type	Description
.xlsx	This is the default type in which all Excel 2007 documents are saved.
.xlsm	This is a basic XML file type that can store VBA macrocode. Macros are sets of Excel commands and instructions grouped together as a single command and a VBA helps us to modify these macros.
.xls	The Excel 97–2003 Workbook option, is used to save the file in a format compatible with many previous versions of Excel.
.xltx/.xltm	.xltx is the default type for a Excel template. It is used while saving a workbook's content, layout, and formatting. .xltm is the default type for a Excel macro-enabled template.
.xlt	This file type enables you to save a Excel template in the Excel 97 through Excel 2003 versions.
.pdf	This file type enables you to save the Excel document as an Adobe PDF (Portable Document Format) file.

The Convert Option

If you open a workbook in .xls format in Excel 2007, a Convert option is added to the Office button. Choose Convert to upgrade the workbook to the Excel 2007 file format.

The Compatibility Checker Feature

If you need to save an XLSX workbook as an XLS spreadsheet for use in another version of Excel, you should be aware that the earlier file version cannot support some of the new features available in Excel 2007. For example, new text and shape effects and SmartArt graphics might be converted to the closest available format to ensure that it is presented consistently. You can use the *Compatibility Checker* feature to identify the compatibility of objects used in your XLSX workbook when it is saved in an earlier version of Excel. In the Microsoft Office Excel - Compatibility Checker dialog box, you can view the features that are not supported in the earlier format and the number of occurrences in the workbook. The objects that are converted cannot be modified.

How to Enter Data and Save a Workbook
Procedure Reference: Create a New Workbook and Enter Data

To create a new workbook and enter data:
1. Click the Office button and choose New to open the New Workbook dialog box.
2. In the New Workbook dialog box, in the Blank And Recent section, verify that Blank Workbook is selected, and then click Create.
3. Click the cell in which you want to enter the data.
4. Type the desired data.
5. Use the appropriate navigation technique to select the next cell where you want to enter data. For example, you can press Enter to move down one cell or Tab to move right one cell.

Procedure Reference: Save a Workbook with the Save As Command

To save a new workbook, or save an existing workbook with a different name, location, or file type:
1. Click the Office button and choose Save As to display the Save As dialog box.
2. In the Save As dialog box, from the Save In drop-down list, navigate to the folder where you want to save the file.
3. In the File Name text box, type a name for the file.
4. From the Save As Type drop-down list, select the desired file format. The default file format in Excel 2007 is XLSX.
5. Click Save.
6. If you save the file in an earlier version of Excel, and there are incompatible contents, the Compatibility Checker will run automatically. If necessary, in the Microsoft Office Excel - Compatibility Checker dialog box, click Continue to convert the features that are not supported in the XLS format to one uneditable object.

Procedure Reference: Save Changes Made to an Existing Workbook

To save changes made to an existing workbook:
1. Open an existing workbook and make some changes.
2. Save the changes.
   - Click the Office button and choose Save.
   - Or, on the Quick Access toolbar, click the Save button.

Using the Compatibility Checker
To run the Compatibility Checker, choose Prepare→Run Compatibility Checker from the Office button menu.

ACTIVITY 1-4

Entering Data and Saving a Workbook

Before You Begin:
Microsoft Office Excel 2007 is open.

Scenario:
You need to document the company's sales and expenditure information for the first quarter in a new Excel spreadsheet. You also need to send a copy of the workbook to a co-worker who is using Excel 2003.

What You Do	How You Do It
1. Create a new, blank workbook.	a. **Click the Office button and choose New.**
	b. In the New Workbook dialog box, **click Create** to open a new, blank workbook.
2. Enter the column headings, *Months, Sales, Expenses,* and *Profit.*	a. **Verify that cell A1 is selected.**
	b. **Type *Months* and press Enter.**
	c. **Select cell B1.**
	d. **Type *Sales* and press Tab.**
	e. In cell C1, **type *Expenses* and press Tab.**
	f. In cell D1, **type *Profit* and press Enter.**
3. Enter the months, sales, and expense values for the first quarter.	a. Use the following graphic to complete the worksheet.

	A	B	C	D
1	Months	Sales	Expenses	Profit
2				
3	Jan	120	115	
4	Feb	195	100	
5	Mar	230	125	
6				

<table>
<tr><td>4.</td><td>Save the workbook as My Ledger.xlsx.</td><td>a.</td><td>Click the Office button and choose Save As to display the Save As dialog box.</td></tr>
<tr><td></td><td></td><td>b.</td><td>If necessary, from the Save In drop-down list, navigate to the C:\084890Data\ Creating a Basic Worksheet folder.</td></tr>
<tr><td></td><td></td><td>c.</td><td>If necessary, in the File Name text box, triple-click to select the default file name.</td></tr>
<tr><td></td><td></td><td>d.</td><td>In the File Name text box, type My Ledger and click Save.</td></tr>
<tr><td>5.</td><td>Check compatibility and save the file in XLS format.</td><td>a.</td><td>Click the Office button and choose Prepare→Run Compatibility Checker.</td></tr>
<tr><td></td><td></td><td>b.</td><td>There should be no compatibility issues. Click OK.</td></tr>
<tr><td></td><td></td><td>c.</td><td>Click the Office button and choose Save As→Excel 97-2003 Workbook.</td></tr>
<tr><td></td><td></td><td>d.</td><td>Verify My Ledger.xls is displayed in the File Name text box and click Save.</td></tr>
<tr><td></td><td></td><td>e.</td><td>Click the Office button and choose Close to close the workbook.</td></tr>
</table>

TOPIC E

Customize the Quick Access Toolbar

You have already been introduced to many of the interface elements of Excel 2007. You now need quick access to some of the options in the various groups on the Ribbon. In this topic, you will customize the Quick Access toolbar to enable such quick access.

Despite the availability of numerous features on the interface, you may need to work with certain features that may be less accessible than others. In order to facilitate access to the features you require, Excel provides options that enable you to display such elements and hide the ones you do not frequently use on the Quick Access toolbar.

How to Customize the Quick Access Toolbar

Procedure Reference: Customize the Quick Access Toolbar

To customize the Quick Access toolbar:

1. Display the Excel Options dialog box.

    ●   Click the Office button and then click Excel options.

    ●   Or, on the Quick Access toolbar, from the Customize Quick Access Toolbar drop-down list, select More Commands.

2. In the Excel Options dialog box, click the Customize category.

3. To add a command on the Quick Access toolbar, from the Choose Commands From drop-down list, select a category.

4. In the list box, select the desired command and click Add. You can use a similar procedure to remove items from the toolbar.

5. If you want to restore the default Quick Access toolbar options, click Reset.

6. If you want to put the Quick Access toolbar below the Ribbon, check Show Quick Access Toolbar Below The Ribbon.

 On the Quick Access toolbar, from the Customize Quick Access Toolbar drop-down list, you can select Show Below The Ribbon to place the Quick Access toolbar below the Ribbon.

7. Click OK to close the Excel Options dialog box.

8. To add a group to the Quick Access toolbar, select the tab on the Ribbon that has the desired group, right-click the name of the group, and choose Add To Quick Access Toolbar.

 You can click the group added to the Quick Access toolbar, right-click a command in it, and choose Add To Quick Access Toolbar to add the shortcut command to the Quick Access toolbar.

ACTIVITY 1-5

Customizing the Quick Access Toolbar

Before You Begin:
Microsoft Office Excel 2007 is open.

Scenario:
You would like to practice adding the shortcut commands to the Quick Access toolbar. You would also like to place the commands in a convenient location.

What You Do	How You Do It
1. **Position the Quick Access toolbar below the Ribbon.**	a. On the Quick Access toolbar, from the Customize Quick Access Toolbar drop-down list, **select Show Below The Ribbon.**
	b. **Verify that the Quick Access toolbar has been moved to appear below the Ribbon.**

2. **Add the Open button to the Quick Access toolbar.**	a. On the Quick Access toolbar, from the Customize Quick Access Toolbar drop-down list, **select More Commands.**
	b. In the Excel Options dialog box, in the list box under the Choose Commands From drop-down list, **scroll down and select Open.**
	c. **Click Add.**
	d. **Click OK** to return to the Excel user interface.

e. **Verify that the Open button appears on the Quick Access toolbar.**

3. **Reset the toolbar to the default settings.**

a. On the Quick Access toolbar, **click the Customize Quick Access Toolbar button and choose More Commands.**

b. In the Excel Options dialog box, **uncheck the Show Quick Access Toolbar Below The Ribbon check box.**

c. **Click Reset** to remove the recently added shortcut command.

d. In the Reset Customizations message box, **click Yes** to restore the toolbar to its default.

e. In the Excel Options dialog box, **click OK.**

Lesson 1 Follow-up

In this lesson, you explored the Microsoft Office Excel 2007 environment. Familiarizing yourself with the Excel environment will help you get started on using the application with ease.

1. How does customizing the Quick Access toolbar help you in your work?

2. What type of work do you do where you use column headings or row headings?

2 | Performing Calculations

Lesson Time: 90 minutes

Lesson Objectives:

In this lesson, you will perform calculations.

You will:

- Create basic formulas.
- Calculate with functions.
- Copy formulas and functions.

Introduction

You have entered labels and numbers into a worksheet to arrange the data in an organized fashion. Now it is time to calculate the data. Microsoft® Office Excel® gives you the flexibility to perform quick calculations that summarizes the row or column data, or if necessary the ability to create formulas that are somewhat more customized. In this lesson, you will perform calculations on existing worksheet data.

Imagine having to manually perform calculations on a worksheet that contains huge volumes of data. Not only would this be tedious and time consuming, but the possibility of introducing errors into the calculations would be significant. Rather than manually calculating information, you can use formulas and functions in Excel to quickly perform calculations on large data sets. This makes the calculation of information quick and efficient and dramatically reduces the possibility of calculation errors.

TOPIC A
Create Basic Formulas

You are familiar with entering data and navigating in a worksheet. You now want to run calculations on data. One method of performing calculations in Excel worksheets is by creating basic formulas. In this topic, you will create basic formulas.

Manual calculation of values in worksheets can be cumbersome, time-consuming, and prone to errors. It is ideal to have an easier and quicker way of calculating values. In Excel, you can create basic formulas to perform calculations on values in worksheets. Creating basic formulas will help you reduce the amount of time it takes to cull valuable information from the data you've entered into a worksheet.

Excel Formulas

Definition:

An Excel *formula* is a set of mathematical instructions that can be used to perform calculations in Excel worksheets. All formulas in Excel begin with an equal sign (=). Excel formulas contain various components, such as functions, references, constants, and operators. A single Excel formula can contain some or all of these components.

Example:

If cell A1 contains the value 2, and cell A2 contains the value 5, you can write a formula that reads =A1+A2 in any cell, and that new cell will contain the result of the calculation: 7.

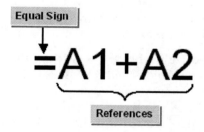

The Formula Bar

The *Formula Bar*, located below the Ribbon, contains the Name Box, formula box, and the Insert Function button. The formula box provides space to accommodate formulas. The Formula Bar also has an option for you to expand or collapse the bar. Additionally, you can resize the Formula Bar and choose to hide it when you are not working with it.

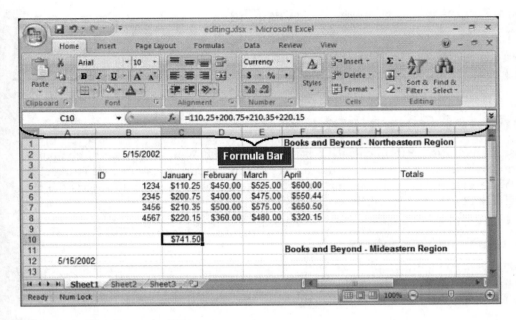

Figure 2-1: *The Formula Bar.*

Elements of an Excel Formula

An Excel formula has various elements.

Formula Element	Description
References	Identifies a <u>cell or a range of cells</u> on a worksheet and refers to the location of the values or data on which you need to apply the formula for calculation.
Operators	Symbols that specify the kind of calculation needed to be performed on the components of a formula.
Constants	Numbers or text values that do not change in the formula. If this value has to change, the formula itself has to be changed.
Functions	Predefined formulas in Excel used to simplify complex calculations.

Common Mathematical Operators

Mathematical operators used in Excel formulas can look different from the ones you are familiar with.

Mathematical Operator	Used For
Plus sign (+)	Addition
Minus sign (−)	Subtraction
Asterisk (*)	Multiplication
Forward slash (/)	Division

Mathematical Operator	Used For
Caret symbol (^)	Exponents
Open and close parentheses ( )	Grouping computation instructions

The Order of Operations

When you use formulas to perform calculations, you need to know the sequence of computations that formulas follow to arrive at the desired result. This order of operations can affect the return value of a formula. When a combination of operators are used, the following is the order in which Excel executes formulas.

1. Computations enclosed in parentheses, wherever they appear in the formula.
2. Computations involving exponents.
3. Computations involving multiplication and division. Because they are equal with regard to the order in which Excel performs them, the operation is performed in the order in which it encounters them, which is from left to right.
4. Computations involving addition and subtraction. Excel also performs them in the order in which it encounters them.

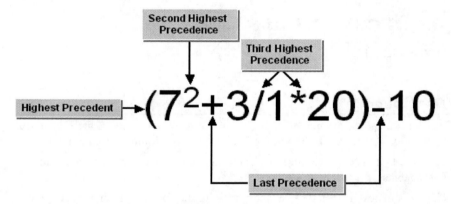

Figure 2-2: *Formulas are processed in a specific order of operations.*

MULTIPLY/DIVIDE THEN ADD + SUBTRACT

( ) OVERRIDE

M
D
A
S

How to Create Basic Formulas

Procedure Reference: Create a Formula

To create a formula:

1. Select the cell in which you will enter the formula.

2. Type the formula.

    *   Type the Equal Sign (=) and then type the cell names with the required arithmetic operators in between.

    *   Or, type the Equal Sign (=) and click the cells that you want to reference with the required arithmetic operators in between.

3. Press Enter to apply the formula and populate the cell with the calculated value.

ACTIVITY 2-1
Creating Basic Formulas

Data Files:

New Ledger.xlsx

Before You Begin:

From the C:\084890Data\Performing Calculations folder, open the New Ledger.xlsx file.

Scenario:

You have a worksheet that tracks the sales revenue generated by sales representatives in your company. The worksheet tracks sales for the months of January, February, and March. Your manager has asked you to calculate the profit for each of the months.

What You Do	How You Do It
1. Calculate the profit for January.	a. **Click cell D2.**
	b. **Type** *=B2–C2*
	c. **Press Enter.**
2. Calculate the profit for the other months.	a. If necessary, **click cell D3.**
	b. In cell D3, **type =**
	c. **Click cell B3 and press Minus Sign (-).**
	d. **Click cell C3 and press Enter.**
3. Calculate the profit for March.	a. **Enter the calculation and verify your result with the following graphic.**

	A	B	C	D
1	Months	Sales	Expenses	Profit
2	Jan	120	115	5
3	Feb	195	100	95
4	Mar	230	125	105
5				

b. **Save the file as *My New Ledger* and leave the file open for the next activity.**

TOPIC B
Calculate with Functions

You have used basic formulas to perform calculations on the data in a worksheet. You now want to explore the built-in functions that Excel provides.

Writing formulas is a very efficient way of performing calculations in a worksheet. However, wouldn't it be nice if you had predefined formulas to run calculations without really having to type them? This would save a lot of time. In Excel, you can calculate using functions. Using functions speeds up the process of performing calculations, because functions are built-in formulas that you do not have to manually construct.

Functions

Definition:

A *function* is a built-in formula in Excel. Functions contain a *function name* followed by *arguments* within parentheses. The function name is the abbreviated name of the function. Functions require arguments, which are the values that the function uses to perform its calculations. The function arguments can be numbers, cell references, constants, formulas, other functions, text, or logical values.

Example:

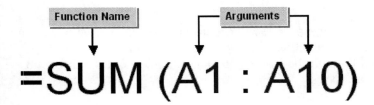

Common Functions in Excel

Excel provides various built-in functions.

Function	Instructs Excel To
SUM	Add all values specified in the argument.
AVERAGE	Calculate the mean average of the values specified in the argument.
MIN	Find the minimum of the values specified in the argument.
MAX	Find the maximum value of the values specified in the argument.
COUNT	Find the number of cells that contain numerical values within the specified range in the argument.
COUNTA	Find the number of cells that contain any data within the specified range. This function does not count the empty cells within the specified range.

The AutoSum( ) Function

The AutoSum( ) function can be directly chosen by selecting AutoSum in the Functions Library group on the Formulas tab. This function can be used to add contiguous numbers in a row or column in a worksheet. The AutoSum drop-down arrow, when clicked, displays a menu with other functions such as Average, Count Numbers, Max, and Min.

The Error Checking Button

The Error Checking button appears next to the cell in which an error is found. It checks for errors in formulas. The first option in the Error Checking menu points out the error. The options in the menu differs according to the type of error tracked. You can ignore the error or edit the formula and update it. The Error Checking button is also found in the Formula Auditing group on the Formulas tab. It displays the Error Checking dialog box, which points out the errors and the various options.

Formula AutoComplete

The *Formula AutoComplete* feature is a dynamic feature in Excel that allows you to conveniently choose and enter formulas and functions. This feature simplifies the task of entering a formula in the formula box or any cell in the worksheet. When you type the equal sign (=) followed by the first letter of a formula, a drop-down list with all available function names beginning with the same character will appear. You can select the required function from the list without having to remember lengthy function names or risk a spelling error.

The Function Library

The *Function Library* is a large command group on the Formulas tab that holds several categories of functions. The various categories of functions are easily accessible on the Function Library, in addition to accessing them through the Insert Function button. The desired function can be selected from these function categories.

The Insert Function Button

The Insert Function button is located in the Function Library group of the Formulas tab and on the Formula Bar. The Insert Function button displays the Insert Function dialog box, which holds numerous functions under several categories. The desired function can be selected and inserted into the selected cell in the worksheet.

How to Calculate with Functions

Procedure Reference: Apply a Formula Using the Formula AutoComplete Feature

To apply a formula using the Formula AutoComplete feature:

1. Select the cell in which you will enter the formula.

2. In the worksheet, type the Equal Sign (=) and the first few letters of the function name.

3. In the displayed AutoComplete drop-down list, double-click a function to select it and enter the formula.

4. Specify the arguments for the function.

5. Close the parentheses and press Enter.

Procedure Reference: Apply a Formula Using the Function Library

To apply a formula using the Function Library:

1. Select the cell in which you will enter the formula.

2. On the Ribbon, select the Formulas tab.

3. In the Function Library group, click Insert Function to display the Insert Function dialog box.

4. In the Select A Function list box, select the desired function and click OK to display the Function Arguments dialog box.

5. In the Function Arguments dialog box, enter the desired arguments and click OK.

ACTIVITY 2-2

Calculating with Functions

Before You Begin:

My New Ledger.xlsx is open.

Scenario:

You would like to calculate the year-to-date sales and expense totals average values for a group of employees. Additionally, you would like the sales data worksheet to reflect the highest and lowest sales and expense totals for each month. You want to calculate these numbers as quickly and efficiently as possible.

What You Do	How You Do It
1. **Calculate the total sales for January through March.**	a. **Click cell B6.**
	b. On the Ribbon, **select the Formulas tab.**
	c. On the Formulas tab, in the Function Library group, **click AutoSum.**
	d. **Select B2:B4.**
	e. **Press Enter** to display the total sales achieved for the first quarter.

2.   Calculate the average sales.

a.   In cell B7, **type** *=av*

b.   In the AutoComplete drop-down list, **double-click Average.**

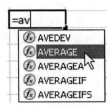

c.   In the worksheet, **select B2:B4.**

d.   **Type)** **and press Enter** to display the sales average.

3. Calculate the highest sales.

a. **Verify cell B8 is selected.**

b. In the Function Library group, **click Insert Function.**

c. In the Insert Function dialog box, in the Select A Function list box, **select Max and click OK.**

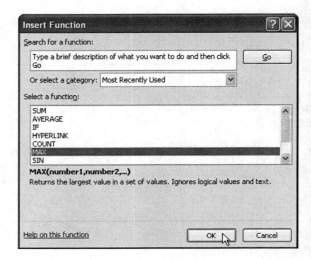

d. **Drag the Function Arguments dialog box away from the worksheet data.**

e. **Select B2:B4.**

f. In the Function Arguments dialog box, **verify that the cell references are displayed in the Number1 text box and click OK.**

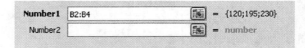

---

4. Calculate the lowest sales.

a. **Click cell B9.**

b. In the Function Library group, **click the AutoSum drop-down arrow, choose Min.**

c. In the worksheet, **select cell B2:B4.**

d. **Press Enter.**

6	Total	545
7	Average	181.6667
8	High	230
9	Low	120
10		

---

5. **Calculate the Total, Average, High and Low for Expenses.**

a. **Use the following graphic to verify your work.**

	A	B	C	D
1	Months	Sales	Expenses	Profit
2	Jan	120	115	5
3	Feb	195	100	95
4	Mar	230	125	105
5				
6	Total	545	340	
7	Average	181.6667	113.3333	
8	High	230	125	
9	Low	120	100	

b. **Save and close the workbook.**

ACTIVITY 2-3
Calculating with Other Basic Functions

Data Files:

Sales Report.xlsx

Before You Begin:

From the C:\084890Data\Performing Calculations folder, open the Sales Report.xlsx file.

Scenario:

You are reviewing the previous year's sales report for your company. The sales report contains the quarterly and total targets achieved by each employee, across regions. The data is not sequentially numbered and, for aesthetic purposes, rows have been inserted after each value. You need a count of employees listed in the worksheet and the total number of employees with region data.

What You Do	How You Do It
1. Find the total number of employees.	a. **Click cell J1 and type** *=cou*
	b. In the AutoComplete drop-down list, **double-click COUNT.**
	c. In the worksheet, **click cell H6.**
	d. **Scroll down and Shift-click cell H106.**
	e. **Type** *)* **and press Enter** to populate cell J1 with the number of employees in the sheet.

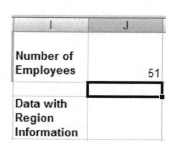

2. **Find the total number of employees with region data.**

   a. In cell J3, **type** *=cou*

   b. In the AutoComplete drop-down list, **double-click COUNTA.**

   c. In the worksheet, **click cell C6.**

   d. **Scroll down and Shift-click cell C106.**

   e. **Type)** **and press Enter** to populate cell J3 with the count of the employees with region information.

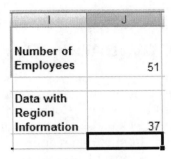

	I	J
	Number of Employees	51
	Data with Region Information	37

   f. **Save the workbook as** *My Sales Report* **and then close it.**

TOPIC C
Copy Formulas and Functions

You have calculated data using formulas and functions. You now need to use the same formulas and functions in multiple cells. In this topic, you will copy formulas and functions.

When working with data in an Excel worksheet, you may find instances where you want to reuse formulas and functions across the worksheet. Rather than manually keying the formulas and functions repeatedly every time you want to reuse them, simply copying and applying them in the required cells will save you time. Excel allows you to copy formulas and functions.

The Cut, Copy, and Paste Options

Excel allows you to move, copy, and paste cells and cell contents in worksheets. After selecting the cell or the cell contents, it can be moved by cutting and pasting. The contents of a cell or a cell can be copied by using the Copy and Paste options. You can access the Cut, Copy, and Paste button from the Clipboard group on the Home tab. You can also access the Cut, Copy, and Paste options from the shortcut menu displayed by right-clicking the selected cell. In addition, you can use shortcut keys to access the Cut, Copy, and Paste options.

The Paste Options

The Paste Options allow you to specify how the copied data should be pasted in the destination cell. Some of the paste options are listed in the following table.

Option	*Description*
Use Destination Theme	Pastes the copied cell using the destination theme.
Match Destination Formatting	Replaces the original formatting of the copied cell and pastes it with the formatting used in the destination cell.
Keep Source Formatting	Retains the original formatting of the copied cell and pastes the data as is.
Values And Number Formatting	Pastes only the values and the number formatting used in the copied cell in the destination cell.
Keep Source Column Width	Retains the column width of the copied cell.
Formatting Only	Pastes only the formatting of the copied cell in the destination cell.
Link Cells	Pastes a link to the copied cells in the destination cells.

Relative References

Definition:

A *relative reference* is a cell reference in a formula that changes when a formula is copied from one position to another, to reflect the new position. Relative references are used to create formulas that use values that are relative and are not fixed. Relative references contain a cell's column and row heading.

Example:

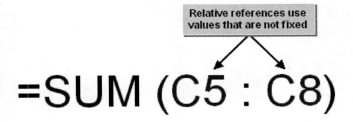

Relative references use values that are not fixed

$$=SUM (C5 : C8)$$

Absolute References

Definition:

An *absolute reference* is a cell reference in a formula that doesn't change when the formula is copied from one position to another to reflect the new position. Absolute references are used in formulas to refer to the values in cells that need to be constant while performing calculations. All absolute references contain a dollar sign ($) before the column and row heading in the cell reference.

Example:

$$=H7* \$H\$3$$

Refers a specific cell and does not change

Conversion of Relative Reference to Absolute Reference

You can select a formula in the formula box and can convert any relative cell reference to an absolute reference by adding a dollar sign ($) in front of the cell's column and row headings.

Mixed References

Definition:

A *mixed reference* is a cell reference that contains both an absolute and a relative reference. When the formula is copied from one place to another, the relative reference in the mixed reference changes while the absolute reference does not change. Mixed references contain either an absolute column and relative row or an absolute row and relative column.

Example:

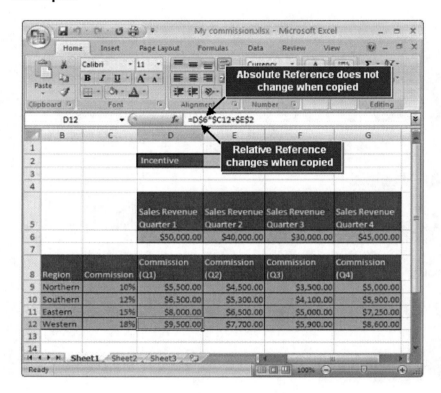

Switch Between Relative, Absolute, and Mixed References

You can change the kind of reference used in a formula if it does not produce the desired result. After selecting the cell that contains the formula, the reference can be changed from the formula box by using the F4 shortcut key to toggle between relative, absolute, and mixed references.

How to Copy Formulas and Functions

Procedure Reference: Copy a Formula or Function

To copy a formula or function:

1. Select the cell that contains the formula you want to copy.
2. On the Home tab, in the Clipboard group, click Copy.
3. Select the destination cell where you want to paste the formula.
4. In the Clipboard group, click Paste.

Procedure Reference: Create an Absolute or Mixed Reference

To create an absolute or mixed reference:

1. Select the cell with the formula that needs to refer to constant cell values.
2. On the Formula Bar, click in the formula box and type the Dollar Sign ($) in front of the column and row references to make the cell value constant in the formula.
3. Press Enter to apply the change made to the formula.

Cut, Copy, and Paste Shortcut Keys

The following table identifies the shortcut keys for the Cut, Copy, and Paste options.

Action	Shortcut Keys
Cut	Ctrl+X
Copy	Ctrl+C
Paste	Ctrl+V

ACTIVITY 2-4
Copying Formulas and Functions

Before You Begin:

From the C:\084890Data\Performing Calculations folder, open the My New Ledger.xlsx file.

Scenario:

Your manager has requested that you add a Totals Summary section to a sales data worksheet you have created. You also need to calculate the average, highest, and lowest sales revenue generated by each employee. You have already created formulas and functions that complete these calculations, and you've decided to reuse the needed formulas and functions to complete your work quickly.

What You Do	How You Do It
1. Copy the Expense Total to Profit Total.	a. Click cell C6.
	b. Select the Home tab.
	c. On the Home tab, in the Clipboard group, **click the Copy button.**
	d. Click cell D6.
	e. In the Clipboard group, **click the Paste button and press Enter.**
	f. **Select and examine the formula in cell C6.**
	g. **Select and examine the formula in cell D6.**
	The copied formula is relative to its new position in the worksheet.
2. Complete the remaining formulas.	a. **Select cells C7:C9.**
	b. In the Clipboard group, **click Copy.**
	c. **Click cell D7, click the Paste button and then press Enter.**
	d. **Save and close the My New Ledger.xlsx file.**

ACTIVITY 2-5

Calculating with an Absolute Reference

Data Files:

Commissions.xlsx

Before You Begin:

From the C:\084890Data\Performing Calculations folder, open the Commissions.xlsx file.

Scenario:

You want to add YTD Commission values to the worksheet to help users quickly identify the total commissions earned by each employee. For each employee, the YTD Commission formula should reference the Commission Rate value specified in the worksheet.

What You Do	How You Do It
1. Calculate the YTD commission for the employees without using an absolute reference for the commission rate.	a. In cell I7, **type the formula =H3*H7 and then press Enter.**
	b. **Copy cell I7.**
	c. **Paste the formula to cells I8:I10**
	d. **Select and examine the copied formulas in I8:I10.**

 The formula used cell H3 as a relative reference in the formula. Cell I9 displays the error #VALUE! because the formula referenced the YTD Total label from cell H5 in the calculation.

2. Modify the formula so that the Commission Rate of 17% is an absolute reference.	a. **Edit the contents of cell I7 to be =H3*H7**

b. **Copy and paste the new formula into cells I8:I10.**

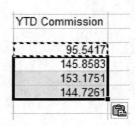

c. **Save the workbook as *My Commissions.xlsx* and close the file.**

Lesson 2 Follow-up

In this lesson, you performed calculations on existing worksheet data. Using Excel's calculation features to perform calculations in worksheets is easier and more efficient than manually performing calculations.

1. **What functions in Excel do you think you will use most often?**

2. **Will you need to use absolute referencing in your formulas back at work? If so, give some examples.**

3 | Modifying a Worksheet

Lesson Time: 60 minutes

Lesson Objectives:

In this lesson, you will modify a worksheet.

You will:

● Manipulate data.

● Insert and delete cells, columns, and rows.

● Work with basic Find & Select options.

● Spell check a worksheet.

Introduction

You are familiar with the Microsoft® Office Excel® environment and have also worked with Excel worksheets. After creating a worksheet, you will undoubtedly want to make changes to it. In this lesson, you will modify the contents of a worksheet.

In order to modify a paper-based spreadsheet, you have to rewrite the entire spreadsheet to include the new additions and other changes. Excel minimizes the effort required to revise and update your spreadsheets. In Excel, you can modify an existing worksheet to update your data rather than create a new worksheet every time you need to change data.

TOPIC A
Manipulate Data

You have entered data and saved it in a workbook. Now, you want to alter the data you have entered. In this topic, you will manipulate data.

You are in the process of creating an expense worksheet for the year. The worksheet has to show, in detail, all the possible expenses for each special day and all months of the year. It also has to be edited and reorganized before finalizing. Using the various Excel options to manipulate large quantities of data will enable you to complete your task more quickly and efficiently.

Undo and Redo

The Undo option allows you to reverse your most recent actions, and the Redo option allows you to cancel your most recent Undo actions. These commands are placed on the Quick Access toolbar. You can also undo several actions at once by selecting the actions to be undone from the Undo drop-down list, which lists all actions recently performed. You can undo and redo up to 100 actions in Excel. However, some actions, such as saving a workbook, cannot be undone. You can also access the Undo and Redo options using the shortcut keys Ctrl+Z and Ctrl+Y, respectively.

Figure 3-1: *The Undo and Redo options.*

Auto Fill

The *Auto Fill feature* fills a cell data or a series of data in a worksheet into a selected range of cells. This is done by entering data into one or more cells and dragging the *fill handle* to the other cells. In order to fill cell data into a selected range, you only need to enter data into a single cell, while data should be entered into two cells to fill it with a series of data. The Starting value for the series should be typed in the first cell and the second value in the next cell to establish the pattern for the series. You can also specify how the selection should be filled using the options in the Auto Fill Options menu.

Fill Handle

The box at the corner of a cell or range that you can use to activate the Excel Auto Fill feature is the *fill handle*. When a cell or range of cells contains data that you can display in increments, drag the fill handle to the left, right, up, or down to fill a range with data, and click the Auto Fill Options button to specify how you want to fill the selection.

Auto Fill Options

The Auto Fill options help you specify how the selected range of cells should be filled.

Auto Fill Option	Description
Copy Cells	Fills the selected range with the selected data in the cell(s).
Fill Series	Fills the selected range with the series of data specified in the selected cell(s).
Fill Formatting Only	Fills the selected range with only the formatting used in the selected cell and not the data.
Fill Without Formatting	Fills the selected range with data in the selected cell but without the formatting applied.

Other Auto Fill Options

The Auto Fill options vary according to the data in the first cell of the selected range of cells. For instance, when a day is typed in the first cell, Auto Fill will have the Fill Days and Fill Weekdays options. By specifying the selection here, the weekend days may be included or excluded from the series as required.

The Copy Cells Option

In the Auto Fill Options button, the Copy Cells option allows you to copy the data to the destination cell or range of cells. The alternative would be to select the cells to copy, click the Copy button, select the cells to paste to, click the Paste button, and continue to paste to every other location. The Copy Cells option simplifies this procedure by allowing the paste to repeat for the duration of the full range.

The Clear Cells Option

The Clear Options button found on the Home tab, in the Cells group, gives you the options to clear the formatting, data, or comments in the cell(s), or you can choose Clear All which will leave the cell blank with all options removed.

How to Manipulate Data

Procedure Reference: Fill Cells with a Series of Data Using Auto Fill

To fill cells with a series of data using Auto Fill:

1. Enter the required data to establish a pattern for the series of data.
2. Select the cell with the value that has helped to establish the pattern.
3. Drag the fill handle to the ending cell of the series.

Procedure Reference: Edit Cell Data

To edit cell data:

1. Select the cell that contains the data you want to edit.
2. Type the new data into the cell and press Enter.

Procedure Reference: Clear Cell Data

To clear cell data:

1. Select the cell.
2. Press the Delete key.

Procedure Reference: Clear a Range

1. Select the range.
2. On the Home tab, in the Editing group, click the Clear button.
3. Choose the appropriate clear option.

Procedure Reference: Move Data Between Cells

To move data between cells:

1. Select the cells that contain data you want to move.
2. Move the selected cells.
   - Position the mouse pointer on the selection border until the mouse pointer changes to a copy/move pointer and drag the selection to the destination.
   - Or, on the Home tab, in the Clipboard group, click the Cut button, select the cell to which you want to move the data, and then click Paste.

ACTIVITY 3-1
Manipulating Data

Data Files:

Editing.xlsx

Before You Begin:

From the C:\084890Data\Modifying a Worksheet folder, open the Editing.xlsx file.

Scenario:

You presented a draft copy of the worksheet that tracks sales data to your manager for her review, and she has suggested a few changes. She wants you to list all the months of the year for both North and Northeast regions. She also wants you to move data and edit some of the current text.

What You Do	How You Do It
1. Add the remaining months of the year for the two regions.	a. Select F4.
	b. **Drag the fill handle to cell N4** to fill the corresponding cells with the remaining months of the year.
	c. Select F15.
	d. **Drag the fill handle to cell N15** to fill the corresponding cells with the remaining months of the year.

2.	Change the Northeast Region label to *East.*	a.	**Click cell F12.** Observe the Formula Bar. The entire label is in the cell.
		b.	**Select cell G12 and examine the Formula Bar.**
		c.	In cell F12, **type *East* and then press Enter.**
		d.	On the Quick Access toolbar, **click Undo.**
		e.	In the Formula box, **double-click Northeast and then type *East***
		f.	**Press Enter.**
3.	In the North Region, **change the Year 2006 label to *Fiscal Year.***	a.	In cell B1, **type *Fiscal Year***
		b.	**Click cell B2 and press the Delete key** to clear the cell.
4.	Clear the Year 2006 labels for the East Region.	a.	**Select A12:A13.**
		b.	On the Home tab, in the Editing group, **click the Clear button.**
		c.	**Select Clear All.**
5.	Move the employee names into column B.	a.	**Select cells A4:A8, and then click Cut.**
		b.	**Select cell B4, and then click Paste.**
		c.	**Select cells A15:A19.**
		d.	**Place the mouse pointer on the selection border until the mouse pointer changes to a Copy/Move pointer.**
		e.	**Place the mouse pointer on the selection border and when it changes to a Copy/Move pointer, click and drag it to B15:B19.**
		f.	**Save as *My Editing.xlsx* and leave the file open for the next activity.**

TOPIC B

Insert and Delete Cells, Columns, and Rows

You have entered data into cells, and you have filled cells with a series of data. Now you want to alter the number of cells, columns, and rows in a worksheet to accommodate changes in your data. In this topic, you will insert and delete cells, columns, and rows.

Imagine you have created an expense statement workbook for the current year. You have forgotten to add the company executive's travel expenses to the workbook. Rather than creating a new workbook to include the new data, you can insert columns, rows, or cells and modify the worksheet. By inserting and deleting cells, columns, and rows, you can modify the layout of a single workbook rather than create a new workbook every time your data requirements change.

Inserting Rows and Columns

You can reorganize your worksheet at anytime by inserting or deleting columns or rows. New rows are added above the selected rows. New columns are added to the left of the selected columns. Any formulas in the workbook are automatically updated to reflect their new location.

How to Insert and Delete Cells, Columns, and Rows

Procedure Reference: Insert or Delete Rows or Columns

To insert or delete a row or column:

1. Select the row(s) or column(s).
2. On the Home tab, in the Cells group, click Insert or Delete.

 The number of row(s) or column(s) selected will be equal to the number of row(s) or column(s) that are inserted or deleted.

Procedure Reference: Insert or Delete a Range of Cells

To insert or delete a range of cells:

1. Select a range of cells.
2. On the Home tab, in the Cells group, click the Insert or Delete drop-down arrow and select Insert Cells or Delete Cells.
3. In the Insert Or Delete dialog box, select the preferred option to shift cells up, down, left, or right, and then click OK.

ACTIVITY 3-2

Inserting and Deleting Columns and Rows

Before You Begin:

My Editing.xlsx is open.

Scenario:

You are the sales executive of a company and have tracked the sales data for the first quarter. You want to add a title to the spreadsheet letting employees know that it is a sales summary. You have decided to add a new column for employee ID numbers and you will need to delete employee Abel because he is no longer in the sales department.

What You Do	How You Do It
1. To make room for a title, **insert four rows above the current row 1 and add the *Sales Summary* title.**	a. **Click the row 1 heading** to select the entire row.
	b. On the Home tab, in the Cells group, **click the Insert drop-down arrow and select Insert Sheet Rows.**

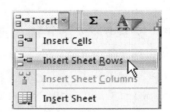

c. **Select rows 1 through 3.**

d. In the Cells group, **click Insert** to insert three rows above the new row.

e. In cell G2, **enter *Sales Summary***

f. **Select and examine the formulas in row 14.** They have adjusted to the new location.

2.	**Insert a new column between columns B and C to make room for the employee IDs.**	a.	**Select column C.**
		b.	In the Cells group, **click Insert.**
		c.	**Select and examine the formulas in columns D through G.** They have adjusted to the new location.

3.	**Enter employee numbers in column C for the North Region.**	a.	**Enter the employee numbers using the following graphic as a guide.**

Employee	ID	January
Willis	1234	$110.25
Abel	2345	$200.75
Binga	3456	$210.35
Culbert	4567	$220.15

4.	**Delete employee Abel's data.**	a.	**Select row 10.**
		b.	In the Cells group, **click Delete.**
		c.	**Save and close the file.**

TOPIC C
Search for Data in a Worksheet

You have worked with rows and columns in a worksheet. You now have a need to locate and change the data in specific cells. In this topic, you will search for data in a worksheet.

You just realized that a piece of data in your worksheet is incorrect. You could search for the data by visually examining each cell starting from the beginning of the worksheet, but that would take a lot of time. Instead, you can use the Find & Select options to locate and change the incorrect data.

In large worksheets, using the Find & Select options is much faster than manually locating data. Additionally, if other instances of the same data exist that you didn't know about, you can change their value as well.

The Find Command

The Find command helps you locate specific data within a worksheet. This command is present in the Find & Select menu, in the Editing group, on the Home tab, and displays the Find And Replace dialog box. The Find tab in the Find And Replace dialog box can also be displayed by using the Ctrl+F shortcut keys.

The Find tab in the Find And Replace dialog box contains various find options that will help you specify the search criteria.

Advanced Find Options

Excel has various advanced search options that are listed in the following table.

Option	Used To
Format button	Search for formats in a worksheet. You can also click the drop-down arrow on the button to access the find format options.
Within drop-down list	Restrict the search to either the active worksheet or to the active workbook.
Search drop-down list	Specify if the search has to be by row or by column.
Look In drop-down list	Specify if the search target should include formulas, values, or comments.
Match Case check box	Specify if the search has to be for the characters with the same casing specified in the Find What text box.
Match Entire Cell Contents check box	Specify if the search has to be for the exact and complete characters that are specified in the Find What text box.

The Replace Command

The Replace command helps you replace the existing data within a worksheet with new data. This command is present in the Find & Select menu, in the Editing group, on the Home tab, and displays the Find And Replace dialog box. The Replace tab in the Find And Replace dialog box can also be displayed using the Ctrl+H shortcut keys.

The Replace tab in the Find And Replace dialog box contains replace options that help you replace data in a worksheet.

Cell Names

In Excel, you can name a cell or a range of cells to identify it by the text you specify rather than by the cell's or range's column and row identification. Cell names are not case sensitive and can be up to 255 characters. When naming a cell, do not use spaces or start with a number. You can use cell names while creating formulas or searching for data in a worksheet. You can also specify the name of the cell in the Name Box and locate the data it represents.

How to Search for Data in a Worksheet

Procedure Reference: Name a Cell

To name a cell:

1. Select the cell you want to name.
2. Click in the Name Box, type the name, and then press Enter.

Procedure Reference: Go to Cell Data

To go to cell data:

1. In the Name Box, type the cell name or cell address.
2. Press Enter.

Procedure Reference: Find and Replace Cell Data

To find cell data:

1. On the Home tab, in the Editing group, click Find & Select and choose Replace.
2. On the Replace tab, in the Find What text box, type the value you want to find.
3. In the Replace With text box, type the replacement data.
4. Click Find Next to find each instance of the value in the workbook, separately.

> Click Find All to locate every instance of the search criteria and populate a list of hyperlinks at the bottom of the Find And Replace dialog box. Click each hyperlink to make that cell active.

5. Replace the text.
    *   Click Replace to replace the selected instance of the search criteria.
    *   Or, click Replace All to replace every instance of the search criteria with the new data.
6. Click Close to return to the worksheet.

ACTIVITY 3-3
Searching for Data in a Worksheet

Data Files:

New Editing.xlsx

Before You Begin:

From the C:\084890Data\Modifying a Worksheet folder, open the New Editing.xlsx file.

Scenario:

You need to update one of the employee ID numbers from 7890 to 1478 and update the last name of the employee whose ID is 3574 to Ferguson. Also, you have two regions that are not as easy to find as the North and East regions, so you would like to name the other two regions to be able to go directly to them without scrolling.

What You Do	How You Do It
1. **Add cell names to the Regions cells.**	a. In the worksheet, **scroll to the right** to view column AF.
	b. **Select cell AF5.**
	c. **Click in the Name Box, type** *South* **and press Enter** to name the cell.
	d. **Select cell AF17.**
	e. **Click in the Name Box, type** *West* **and press Enter** to name the cell.
2. **Go directly to the various regions without scrolling.**	a. **Press Ctrl+Home.**
	b. In the Name Box, **type** *South* **and press Enter.**
	c. **Press Ctrl+Home.**
	d. In the Name Box, **type** *West* **and press Enter.**

3. **Replace employee ID 7890 with *1478.***

   a. On the Home tab, in the Editing group, **click Find & Select and choose Replace** to display the Find And Replace dialog box.

   b. In the Find What text box, **type *7890***

   c. In the Replace With text box, **type *1478***

   d. **Click Find Next** to locate the cell containing employee ID 7890.

   e. **Click Replace** to update Hoffman's employee ID.

   f. **Click Close** to close the Find And Replace dialog box.

4. **Update the employee name for ID 3574 to *Ferguson.***

   a. In the Editing group, **Click Find & Select, and choose Find.**

   b. In the Find What text box, **type *3574* and click Find Next.**

   c. **Click Close.**

   d. In cell AA23, **type *Ferguson* and press Enter.**

   e. **Save the file as *My New Editing.xlsx* and then close the file.**

TOPIC D
Spell Check a Worksheet

You have revised your worksheet data. Now you want to make sure that there are no spelling errors in the worksheet. In this topic, you will spell check a worksheet.

You are working on your expense worksheet. As a final step in the process before you submit it to your manager, you want to verify the spelling of the text in the file. By spell checking your worksheet, you can correct any misspelled words.

The Spelling Dialog Box

The Spelling dialog box displays spelling mistakes or words that Excel does not recognize in the worksheet. You can display the Spelling dialog box using the F7 shortcut key or by accessing it in the Proofing group on the Review tab.

The Spelling dialog box is used to spell check a worksheet.

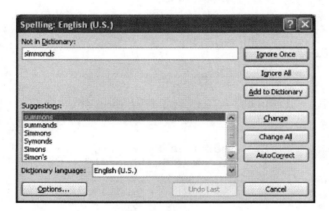

Figure 3-2: The Spelling dialog box.

Spell Check Options	Description
Ignore Once	Ignore the current occurrence
Ignore All	Ignore all occurrences
Add to Dictionary	Add the word to dictionary
Change	Change the current occurrence of word with correct word.
Change All	Replace all occurrences of the word.
Undo Last	Reverse most recent action.
Options	Display Excel option dialog box.
Dictionary Language	Options for language selection.

How to Spell Check a Worksheet

Procedure Reference: Spell Check a Worksheet

To spell check a worksheet:

1. On the Ribbon, select the Review tab.

2. On the Review tab, in the Proofing group, click Spelling.

3. In the Spelling dialog box, address the words that are flagged as being misspelled in the worksheet.

    *   To overlook the misspelled word, click Ignore Once or Ignore All.

    *   Click Add To Dictionary to denote it as a correctly spelled word and add it to the dictionary.

    *   Correct the misspelled words by selecting the correct word in the Suggestions list box and then clicking Change or Change All.

 Click AutoCorrect to correct all occurrences of the misspelled word in the Not In Dictionary text box automatically. This will correct the word automatically across worksheets and workbooks.

4. In the Microsoft Office Excel message box, click OK to confirm the completion of the spell checking process.

ACTIVITY 3-4

Spell Checking a Worksheet

Data Files:

Travel Expenses.xlsx

Before You Begin:

From the C:\084890Data\Modifying a Worksheet folder, open the Travel Expenses.xlsx file.

Scenario:

You have created a travel expenses worksheet for your manager. Before submitting the worksheet to your manager, you would like to check the contents of the worksheet for any misspelled words.

What You Do	How You Do It
1. **Correct all occurrences of misspelled words across the worksheet.**	a. On the Ribbon, **select the Review tab.** b. On the Review tab, in the Proofing group, **click Spelling.**
	c. In the Spelling: English (U.S.) dialog box, in the Suggestions list box, **select Parking.**

d. **Click Change** to replace the misspelled word.

e. **Click Change** to correct telephone.

f. **Click Change All** to replace all occurrences of the misspelling of parking.

g. **Click Change** to correct entertainment.

h. In the Microsoft Office Excel message box, **click OK** to confirm the completion of the spell checking process.

i. **Save the workbook as *My Travel Expenses* and close the file.**

Lesson 3 Follow-up

In this lesson, you modified a worksheet. Modifying a worksheet lets you update existing data to suit your requirements, rather than creating a new worksheet every time your data changes.

1. **Consider a worksheet you are either already using at work or one you need to create from scratch. How might you modify the existing worksheet to meet your current business needs?**

2. **Consider the methods Excel offers to find data. Which do you think you will use?**

4 | Formatting a Worksheet

Lesson Time: 60 minutes

Lesson Objectives:

In this lesson, you will format a worksheet.

You will:

- Modify fonts.
- Add borders and color to cells.
- Change column width and row height.
- Apply number formats.
- Align cell contents.
- Apply cell styles.

Introduction

You have performed calculations on a worksheet that contains values. You now want to define specific areas of your worksheet to make it easier to visually locate data. In this lesson, you will format a worksheet.

A worksheet should be easy to interpret and visually appealing. Formatting a worksheet will improve its aesthetic appeal and help avoid data cluttering. By applying Excel formats, you can visually differentiate one set of data from another, making it easier to locate and analyze information.

TOPIC A
Modify Fonts

You have created basic worksheets and now want to make it easier to visually locate data in a worksheet. One way of doing this is by changing the font size and type for specific pieces of data. In this lesson, you will modify fonts.

The headlines in a newspaper are always larger and more striking than the text of the news stories. The headlines make it easy to scan through and locate important news. Similarly, changing the font size and type of specific portions of your worksheet helps highlight information. By modifying fonts, you can change the appearance of your data, making it easier to read and locate critical information.

Fonts

Definition:

A *font* is a predefined typeface that can be used for formatting characters. Each font has a unique style and character spacing. Fonts can be built-in or user-defined. Typeface can be alphabets, numerals, punctuation marks, ideograms, and symbols.

Example:

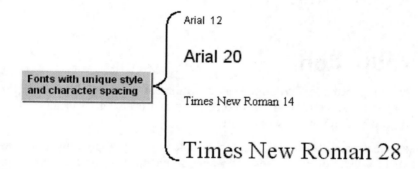

The Font Group

The Font group on the Home tab contains various font formatting options. You can also access these options from the Format Cells dialog box.

The Format Cells Dialog Box

The Format Cells dialog box contains various formatting options. This dialog box can be displayed by the Dialog Box Launcher button, in the Alignment group or Number group, on the Home tab.

Options in the Format Cell dialog box are used to enhance a workbook.

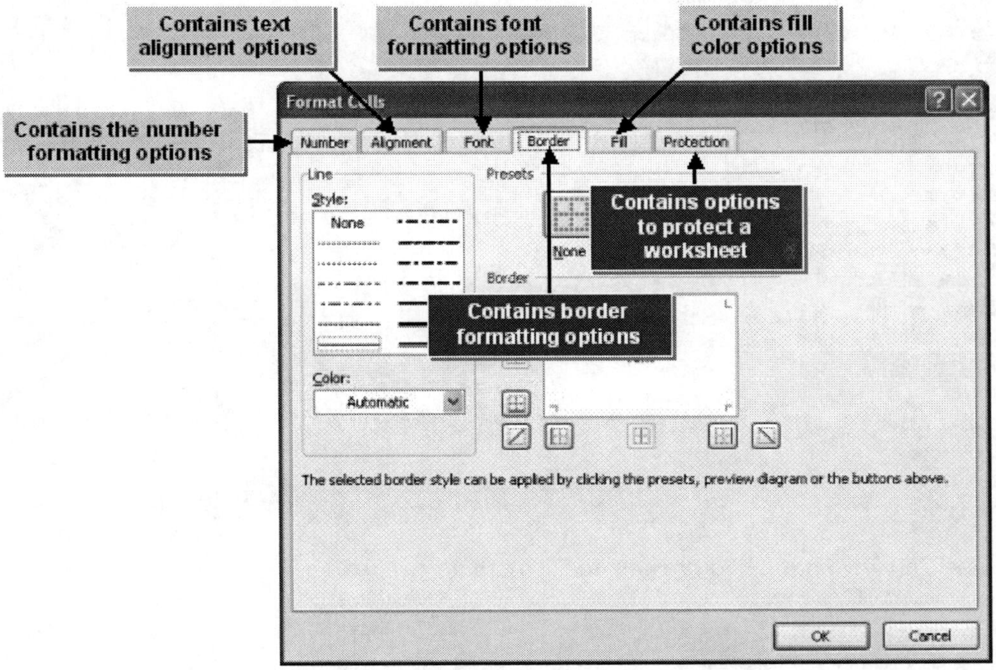

Figure 4-1: The Format Cell dialog box.

Galleries

A *gallery* is a repository for elements of the same category. A gallery acts as a central location for accessing the various styles and appearance settings for an object. Excel provides various galleries for cell styles, tables, shapes, and even charts. The large availability of preset formats and styles makes it easy to quickly alter any graphical object.

Live Preview

Live Preview is a dynamic feature that allows you to preview how formatting options will look on a worksheet before you actually apply the selected formatting. For example, when any font is moused over, you can actually see a live preview of how it will affect the appearance of the selected object without actually applying the font to the object. The temporary formatting is removed when the mouse pointer is moved away.

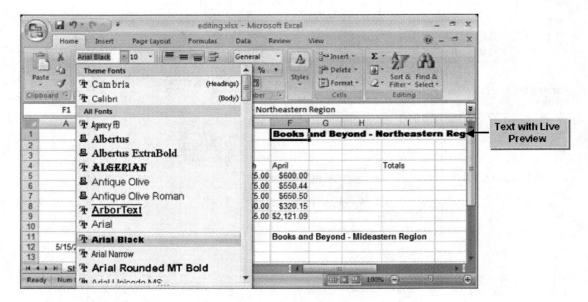

Figure 4-2: *Live Preview enables to preview the formatting options.*

How to Modify Fonts, Size and Style
Procedure Reference: Change the Font Type, Size, or Style

To change the font type, size, or style

1. Select the cell(s) that you want to format.

2. Change the font type, size, and style in the worksheet.

    *   On the Home tab, in the Font group, click the Font drop-down arrow and select the desired font.

    *   Click the Font Size drop-down arrow and select the desired font size.

    *   If desired, click the Bold, Italic, and Underline buttons.

    *   Change the font type using the Mini toolbar.

        a. Right-click the cell(s) with the data to be formatted.

        b. On the Mini toolbar, select the desired font, size, and style.

ACTIVITY 4-1
Modifying Fonts

Data Files:

Calculations.xlsx

Before You Begin:

From the C:\084890Data\Formatting a Worksheet folder, open the Calculations.xlsx file.

Scenario:

You are involved in the process of preparing the sales report for the year. After populating all the data, you feel that you need to enhance the worksheet to easily locate data and also make it more visually appealing. All your company reports follow the Verdana font style, and you want to update your workbook accordingly. You also want all the headings in the worksheet to stand out from the remaining data.

What You Do	How You Do It
1. Change the font of the data in the entire worksheet to Verdana.	a. **Click the Select All button** to select the entire worksheet.
	b. On the Home tab, in the Font group, in the Font drop-down list, **scroll down and place the mouse pointer over Verdana.**
	c. **Preview the selected font that is now displayed in the worksheet.**
	d. **Select Verdana.**

2. Convert the size of the main heading to 16.

   a. **Click cell A1.**

   b. In the Font group, from the Font Size drop-down list, **select 16.**

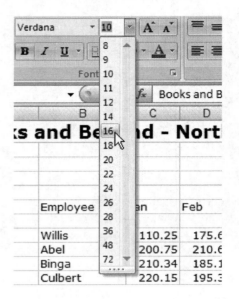

3. Change the font size of the other headings in the worksheet to 12.

   a. **Select rows 5 and 6.**

   b. **Hold down Ctrl and select row 20, cells B13:B14 and B16:B:17.**

   c. From the Font Size drop-down list, **select 12** to change the size of the selected headings.

4. Apply the Bold format to the Totals Summary heading.

   a. **Click cell B20.**

   b. In the Font group, **click the Bold button.**

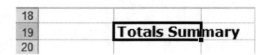

   c. **Save the workbook as *My Calculations* and leave it open for the next activity.**

TOPIC B
Add Borders and Color to Cells

You modified fonts in a worksheet, making it easier to visually locate data. Another method of highlighting data is by applying borders and colors to cells. In this topic, you will add borders and color to cells.

Sign boards with attractive colors and lights help customers quickly locate shops. Similarly, adding borders and colors to cells in your worksheet will help you quickly locate critical information.

Border Options

Border options are used to apply borders to cells. Excel provides you with options to apply a border to some or all the sides of a cell or a range of cells. You can access border options from the Border drop-down list in the Font group or from the Border tab in the Format Cells dialog box. The border line style and color can also be specified in the Format Cells dialog box. Alternatively, you can apply a new or different border style using the preset border styles available in the Border drop-down list or draw borders using the tools in the Draw Borders section.

The Border tab of the Format Cells dialog box contains various border options.

Border Options	Contains
Line section	The Style list box and the Color drop-down list. This will allow you to specify the desired border style and border color for the selected cell.
Presets Section	Buttons that will allow you to apply the selected border style to the cell. The None button will remove borders.
Border Section	Buttons that will allow you to apply the selected border style to the cell. You can apply the selected border style by either clicking the presets or by clicking the preview diagram or the border buttons in this section.

Sheet Background

Excel allows you to apply a background to an entire worksheet. The background can be a picture. The Background button, in the Page Setup group, on the Ribbon, displays the Sheet Background dialog box from which the background to be applied can be selected. The Background button acts as a toggle button. Once a background is added to a worksheet, it can be removed using the same button.

You can also apply any desired color or pattern as a background to the entire worksheet by using the Fill Color gallery or the options in the Fill tab of the Format dialog box.

Fill Tab Option	Used To
Background Color Section	Select the desired color for the background.

Fill Tab Option	Used To
Pattern Color drop-down list	Select the desired pattern color.
Pattern Style drop-down list	Select the desired pattern style.
More Colors button	Display the Colors dialog box wherein you can specify either a standard or custom color for the background.
Fill Effects button	Display the Fill Effects dialog box from which the desired effect can be selected for the background.

Paste Options

The paste options in Excel enable you to paste the entire copied selection or only formulas or values. You can paste all except borders, transpose the data, or paste as a link. All of these options are also available from the Paste Special dialog box. Additionally, within the Paste Special dialog box you can perform mathematical operations with values in the destination cells. The paste options are located on the Paste drop-down list in the Clipboard group on the Home tab.

How to Add Borders and Color to Cells

Procedure Reference: Add Background Color

To add background color:

1. Select the cell(s) or the entire worksheet to add a background color.

2. Add a desired background color.

   - On the Home tab, in the Font group, click the Fill Color drop-down arrow and, in the Fill Color gallery, select the desired color.

   - Display the Format Cells dialog box, select the Fill tab, select the desired color in the Background Color section, and then click OK to apply the color to the selected cells or the worksheet.

   - Or, right-click the selected cells, and on the displayed Mini toolbar, click the Fill Color drop-down arrow and select the color.

Procedure Reference: Add Borders to Cells

To add borders to cells:

1. Select the cell(s) that need borders.

2. Apply a border to the selected cells.

   - On the Home tab, in the Font group, click the Border drop-down arrow, select the desired border.

   - Display the Format Cells dialog box, select the Border tab, and set the desired border.

     a. In the Line section, select the desired border style.

     b. In the Color section, select the desired border color from the Color gallery.

     c. In the Presets and Border sections, set the borders for the selected cells and preview the border.

d.   Click OK.

- Or, right-click the selected cell(s), and on the displayed Mini toolbar, click the Border drop-down arrow and select the desired border.

Procedure Reference: Remove Cell Borders

To remove cell borders:

1.   In the worksheet, select the cells from which the borders need to be removed.

2.   Remove the border.

- On the Home tab, in the Font group, click the Border drop-down arrow and choose No Border.

- Display the Format Cells dialog box, select the Border tab, click None in the Presets section, and then click OK.

- Or, right-click the selected cell(s) and on the displayed Mini toolbar, click the Border drop-down arrow and choose No Border.

ACTIVITY 4-2
Adding Borders and Colors to Cells

Before You Begin:
My Calculations.xlsx is open.

Scenario:
You are still in the process of formatting your sales report and want to draw attention to specific regions of the worksheet. You have decided to highlight the Total summary and YTD regions using a bright color. You also want to draw a box around the Totals Summary region to emphasize the section even more.

What You Do	How You Do It
1. **Add a bright-colored background to the YTD region.**	a. **Select cells H5:L11.**
	b. On the Home tab, in the Font group, **click the Fill Color drop-down arrow.**
	c. In the Fill Color gallery, in the Standard Colors section, **select the Yellow color.**

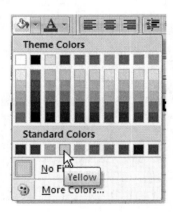

2. Add the same background to the Totals Summary region.

    a. In the Clipboard group, **click the Copy button.**

    b. **Scroll down and select cells B20:C27.**

    c. In the Clipboard group, **click the Paste drop-down arrow and choose Paste Special.**

    d. In the Paste Special dialog box, in the Paste section, **select the Formats option and click OK.**

---

3. Add a border around the Totals Summary region of the worksheet.

    a. With B20:C27 selected, in the Font group, **click the Dialog Box Launcher button.**

    b. In the Format Cells dialog box, **select the Border tab** to view the border options.

    c. In the Line section, in the Style list box, in the second column, **select the thickest style.**

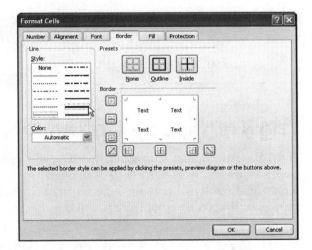

    d. In the Presets section, **click Outline and then click OK.**

    e. **Click any cell outside the selected region** to deselect it so you can see the border.

    f. **Save and close the workbook.**

TOPIC C
Change Column Width and Row Height

You have emphasized specific portions of data by adding borders and color to cells. You now want the data stored in the columns and rows to fit in their respective cells. In this topic, you will change the width of columns and the height of rows.

It would be difficult to work in a worksheet in which the data is obscured by rows that are too short or columns that are too narrow. This would also take away the visual appeal of your worksheet. By changing the column width and row height, the data stored in the columns and rows can be fit into their respective cells and your data will display as you intend it to.

Methods for Changing Column Width and Row Height

There are several methods to adjust column width and row height in Excel. You can,

● Automatically adjust column width and row height using the AutoFit option.

● Manually adjust column width and row height to fit the contents.

● Or, set specific column width and row height.

 Excel displays ## signs in cells when the numeric data is too wide to be displayed within the current column width. When the column width is adjusted, the # signs will disappear, and the numbers will be displayed.

The Transpose Option

The Transpose option automatically shifts the vertical and horizontal orientation of columns and rows on the worksheet. For example, if the data is set up with the months as rows and the department names as columns, the transpose option will reverse the rows and columns. The months will become columns and the department names will become rows.

The Row and Column Hide Options

The row and column hide options can be accessed from the Format menu in the Cells group on the Home tab. The Hide option allows you to hide any columns or rows in a worksheet. Though hidden, the columns and rows still exist in the worksheet but are not visible to the user unless they are unhidden. The Unhide option is used to make any columns or rows you have previously hidden visible. You can also access the Hide and Unhide commands from the shortcut menu that is displayed when a column or row is selected.

How to Change Column Width and Row Height

Procedure Reference: Transpose Data

To transpose data during paste:

1. Select the data.

2. Copy the selected cells.

3. Select the cell destination in which the copied content will be pasted to.

4. On the Home tab, in the Clipboard group, click the Paste drop-down arrow and choose Transpose.

Procedure Reference: Change Column Width and Row Height

To change column width and row height by dragging boundaries:

1. Change the column width or row height.

    *   Change column width or row height to a specific value.

        a. Select the column or row you want to change.

        b. Right-click the selection and choose Column Width or Row Height, or on the Home tab, in the Cells group, click Format and choose Column Width or Row Height.

        c. In the Column Width or Row Height dialog box, in the Column Width or Row Height text box, type a new value for the column width or row height.

        d. Click OK to change the column width or row height.

    *   Manually adjust column width or row height, by dragging to the left or right to adjust the column width or by dragging up or down to adjust the row height as needed.

    *   Or, AutoFit column width or row height, by double-clicking the border between the two column or two row headings.

Procedure Reference: Hide or Unhide Columns or Rows

To hide columns or rows:

1. Select the column(s) or row(s) you want to hide or unhide.

     To select hidden rows or columns, select a range that includes the visible rows or columns on either side of the hidden rows or columns. In the worksheet, if the first row or column is hidden, you can select it by typing A1 in the Name Box. Additionally, you can select the first row or column by using the same method in the Go To dialog box.

2. Hide or unhide the selected column(s) or row(s).

    *   On the Home tab, in the Cells group, from the Format drop-down list, choose Hide & Unhide→Hide Columns or Unhide Columns or Hide & Unhide→Hide Rows or Unhide Rows.

    *   Or, right-click anywhere in the selected column(s) or row(s) and choose Hide or Unhide.

ACTIVITY 4-3
Transposing Data and Adjusting Column Width

Data Files:

Company Results.xslx

Before You Begin:

From the C:\084890Data\Formatting a Worksheet folder, open the Company Results.xlsx file.

Scenario:

You have just received your company's quarterly sales results worksheet that displays each quarter in a column. You would like to generate a report where the quarters are displayed in rows. As you are left with very little time to prepare the report, you cannot waste time by manually typing the values. Once the report is generated, you will hide the original data before considering it to be final.

What You Do	**How You Do It**
1. **Transpose the column and row contents while pasting the contents to a new location.**	a. **Select cells A4:D12.**
	b. On the Home tab, in the Clipboard group, **click the Copy button.**
	c. **Select cell A15.**
	d. In the Clipboard group, **click the Paste drop-down arrow and select Transpose.**
	e. **Verify that the content is transposed and pasted.** The project information now appears in columnar format.
2. **Increase the width of columns F, G, and I.**	a. **Position the mouse pointer at the border between columns F and G, and then drag the border to the right until the data is visible in column F.**
	b. **Double-click the border between columns G and H to autofit the content in column G.**

c. **Adjust the width of column I to display its contents.**

Development	Leased space		Grand Totals
639000	576000		10092000
779000	596000		11115000
140000	20000		1023000

3. **Hide rows 4:12.**

a. **Select rows 4:12.**

b. In the Cells group, **click Format, and then choose Hide & Unhide→Hide Rows.**

c. **Examine the row headings.** Since rows 4 through 12 are hidden, the worksheet shows row 3 followed by row 13.

d. **Save as *My Company Results.xlsx* and close the file.**

TOPIC D
Apply Number Formats

You have formatted text and altered column width in a worksheet. You now want to format numeric data in the worksheet. In this topic, you will apply number formats.

You have an inventory worksheet that has a column for value of the stock. Rather than manually entering dollar sign ($) when you enter the stock value, you will apply number format to this column so that the entered number is displayed in currency format. Applying number formats changes the appearance of numeric data, making it easier to identify the type of data within cells.

Number Formats

Definition:

A *number format* is a data format that changes the appearance of the numerical data in a cell. Each number format applies specialized formatting on the data. Only the appearance of the data in a cell changes, not the data itself. You can apply a number format to a cell or a range of cells before or after you type in the numerical data. Number formats applied can vary according to the type of data, such as currency, date, or time.

Example:

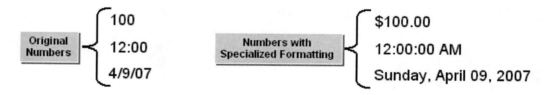

Number Formats in Excel

Excel's pre-installed number formats come in a variety of categories. They can be accessed from the Number tab of the Format Cells dialog box and also from the Number group on the Home tab.

Number Format Category	Used For
General	Default number formatting that Excel applies when you type a number. No decimals are displayed.
Number	Displaying numbers. You can specify the number of decimal places and the way the negative numbers need to be displayed.
Currency	Displaying monetary values. The default currency symbol with numbers will be displayed.
Accounting	Monetary values. This will also align the currency symbols and decimal points of numbers in a column.
Date	Displaying date and time serial numbers as date values. The type and the language setting that you want can be specified to display date and time in other language formats.

Number Format Category	Used For
Time	Displaying date and time serial numbers as time values. The type and the language setting that you want can be specified to display the date and time in other language formats.
Percentage	Multiplying the cell value by 100 and displaying the result with a percent symbol.
Fraction	Displaying a number as a fraction, according to the type of fraction that you specify.
Scientific	Displaying a number in exponential notation.
Text	Treating the content of a cell as text. Even when numbers are typed, this will display the content exactly as you type it. Use if leading zeros are necessary, as in an employee number.
Special	Displaying a number as a postal code (zip code), phone number, or Social Security number.
Custom	Modifying a copy of an existing number format code to create a custom number format.

Custom Number Formats

Excel allows you to create your own custom number formats. Custom number formats can be created when Excel's predefined number format categories do not provide the suitable format required for a particular type of numerical data. When creating a custom number, the # symbol is used to indicate that only significant digits will be displayed and insignificant zeros will not be displayed. Quotation marks, at the beginning and end of text, are used to indicate how the text should be displayed with the custom number. You can add between 200 and 250 number formats to the list.

How to Apply Number Formats

Procedure Reference: Apply Number Formats

To apply number formats:

1. Select the cell(s) to which you want to apply a number format.
2. Select the number format.
   - On the Home tab, in the Number group, select the desired number format and number of decimal places.
   - Or, display the Format Cells dialog box, select the Number tab, select the desired number format and number of decimal places category in the Category list box, and then click OK to apply the number format.

Procedure Reference: Create a Custom Number Format

To create a custom number format:

1. Select the cell(s) to which you want to apply the custom number format.
2. Display the Format Cells dialog box and select the Number tab.
3. In the Category list box, select Custom.

4. Define the new custom format.

- In the Type text box, type and define a new custom format.
- Or, in the Type list box, select one of the existing models and modify it in the Type text box.

5. Click OK to apply the format.

ACTIVITY 4-4
Applying Number Formats

Data Files:

New Calculations.xlsx

Before You Begin:

From the C:\084890Data\Formatting a Worksheet folder, open the New Calculations.xlsx file.

Scenario:

You want each monetary value in the sales report to have no more than two decimal places and to have a dollar notation to represent U.S. dollars. You also need to display the current date in the worksheet with the format *day-month-year*. You have been asked to format the employee ID numbers using standard company guidelines.

What You Do	How You Do It
1. **Apply the dollar currency format to the sales data.**	a. **Select cells C8:F17.**
	b. On the Home tab, in the Cells group, **click Format and choose Format Cells.**
	c. In the Format Cells dialog box, on the Number tab, in the Category list box, **select Currency.**
	d. **Click OK** to apply the formatting.

Jan	Feb	Mar	Apr
$110.25	$175.65	$140.96	$135.15
$200.75	$210.63	$240.82	$205.79
$210.34	$185.11	$195.14	$310.44
$220.15	$195.37	$185.66	$250.15
$741.49	$766.76	$762.58	$901.53
$185.37	$191.69	$190.65	$225.38
$220.15	$210.63	$240.82	$310.44
$110.25	$175.65	$140.96	$135.15

2. Apply the dollar currency format to the sales data in the Totals Summary and YTD regions.

a. **Scroll down and select cells C22:C27.**

b. **Right-click the selected cells, select Format Cells, and then on the Number tab, select Currency, and click OK.**

c. **Adjust the width of column C to fit the contents.**

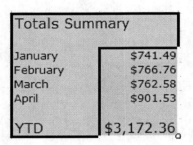

Totals Summary	
January	$741.49
February	$766.76
March	$762.58
April	$901.53
YTD	$3,172.36

d. **Select cells H8:L11, and then apply the dollar currency format to the range of cells.**

3. Enter today's date and change the format.

a. **Click cell A2.**

b. **Enter today's date.**

c. **Right-click cell A2 and choose Format Cells.**

d. In the Type list box, **select 14-Mar-01 and click OK** to apply this date format to the selected cell.

4. Create the custom number format for the employee IDs.

a. **Select A8:A11.**

b. **Right-click the selected cells and choose Format Cells** to display the Format Cells dialog box.

c. On the Number tab, in the Category list box, **select Custom.**

d. In the Type text box, **double-click and type "ID"-##-##**

e. **Click OK to apply the formatting.**

f. **Verify that the employee ID appears in the newly created format.**

8	ID-12-34
9	ID-23-45
10	ID-34-56
11	ID-45-67

g. **Save the file as *My New Calculations.xlsx* and leave the file open for the next activity.**

TOPIC E
Position Cell Contents

You have formatted cells and numeric data in a worksheet to enhance the presentation of data in the cells. By controlling the positioning of the text in a cell, you can further enhance the presentation of content in cells. In this topic, you will align cell contents.

When a single piece of data stretches across multiple cells, you can make it easier on yourself to manage that data by merging all of those cells into a single, larger cell. Merging cells will help you manage data better and will improve the appearance of your worksheet.

Aligning cell content will give your worksheets a neat and professional look. Using the alignment options in Excel, you can reposition the contents of specific cells to align them with the rest of the data in a worksheet. This will improve the visual appeal of the worksheet.

Alignment Options

Alignment options are used to align cell contents horizontally or vertically. The alignment option will position the data based on the height and width of the cell. The following table lists the alignment options.

Alignment Option	*Used To*
Top Align	Align text to the top of the cell.
Middle Align	Align text to the center between the top and bottom of the cell.
Bottom Align	Align text to the bottom of the cell.
Align Text Left	Align text to the left within the cell.
Center	Align text to the center within the cell.
Align Text Right	Align text to the right within the cell.
Decrease Indent	Decrease the indent between the left border and the text within the cell.
Increase Indent	Increase the indent between the left border and the text within the cell.
Orientation	Rotate the text within the cell vertically or diagonally.

The Cell Merge Options

The cell merge options in Excel allow you to merge cells across columns and rows and also to split cells that have been merged. You can directly merge cells using the Merge & Center button or specify the desired option from the Merge & Center drop-down list. You can also merge cells using the Merge Cells check box on the Alignment tab of the Format Cells dialog box.

The Merge & Center drop-down list contains various merge options.

Merge Option	*Description*
Merge & Center	Combines the selected cells to a larger single cell and then centers the data.

Merge Option	Description
Merge Across	Combines the selected cells across columns to a larger single cell. Multiple rows of data can be selected and will be retained.
Merge Cells	Combines the selected cells across columns to a larger single cell. Only the data in the upper-left cell will be retained.
Unmerge Cells	Splits the cell that has been merged to separate cells.

The Merge & Center Button

The Merge & Center button, in the Alignment group, on the Home tab, is used to merge cells or split cells that have been merged into separate cells. This button functions like a toggle.

Wrap Text

Excel enables you to automatically wrap data within a cell using the Wrap Text option. This option moves content to the next line within a cell if the content extends beyond the boundaries of the cell. The Wrap Text button in the Alignment group and the Wrap Text check box on the Alignment tab enable this option.

Manual Line Breaks

The contents in a cell can also be wrapped within a cell by entering a manual line break. After locating the point at which the line needs to be broken, a manual line break can be inserted by pressing the Alt+Enter key combination.

How to Align or Merge Cell Contents

Procedure Reference: Align Cell Contents

To align cell contents:

1. Select the cell(s) whose contents you want to align.
2. Align the contents of the selected cell(s).
   - Align text within cells using the align buttons in the Alignment group on the Home tab.
   - Or, right-click the selected cells and on the displayed Mini toolbar, click the desired align buttons.

Procedure Reference: Merge or Split Cells

To merge or split cells:

1. Select the range of contiguous cells you want to merge or split.
2. Merge or split the selected cells.
   - On the Home tab, in the Alignment group, click the Merge & Center drop-down arrow and select the desired merge option.
   - Display the Format Cells dialog box, select the Alignment tab, check or uncheck the Merge Cells check box in the Text Control section, and then click OK.
   - Or, right-click the selected range of cells, and on the displayed Mini toolbar, click the Merge & Center button.

Procedure Reference: Wrap Cell Contents

To wrap cell contents:

1. Select the cells in which the content needs to wrap.

2. Wrap text in the selected cells.

    - On the Home tab, in the Alignment group, click the Wrap Text button.

    - Or, display the Format Cells dialog box, select the Alignment tab, and check the Wrap Text check box and click OK.

ACTIVITY 4-5
Positioning Cell Contents

Before You Begin:
My New Calculations.xlsx is open.

Scenario:
You are working on the sales data worksheet to get it ready for a presentation. You notice that the headings in the sales data worksheet are not aligned with the numbers that appear below them. The labels are left aligned, but the numbers are right aligned. You want them aligned similarly. The title of the worksheet spans several cells and the Totals Summary title spans two cells, and you want each of the titles to be contained in one cell for formatting flexibility. Also, you would like the Commission Rate text to wrap so that it is contained in a single cell.

What You Do	How You Do It
1. Right align the column headings in rows 5 and 6.	a. Select rows 5 and 6.
	b. On the Home tab, in the Alignment group, **click the Align Text Right button** to right align the contents of the row.

2. Merge the cells with the Books and Beyond heading into a single cell.	a. Select A1:F1.
	b. In the Alignment group, **click the Merge & Center drop-down arrow** and **select Merge Cells.**
3. Merge and center the Totals Summary heading in a single cell.	a. Select B20:C20.
	b. In the Alignment group, **click the Merge & Center button.**

4. **Wrap the contents of the Commission Rate label into a single cell.**

a. **Select cell F3 and examine the contents of the cell.**

b. **Right-click and select Format Cells.**

c. On the Alignment tab, in the Text Control section, **check the Wrap Text check box and then click OK.**

d. **Save the file.**

TOPIC F
Apply Cell Styles

You have formatted worksheets using many formatting options. Now you would like to create a consistent look to all your worksheets. You will use cell styles to format your worksheet.

In order to attract the attention of readers, magazines use attractive colors and styles to present articles and their title pages. Similarly applying cell styles will enhance your worksheets by developing their visual appeal, making them very attractive and interesting.

Cell Styles

Definition:

A *cell style* is a predefined set of appearance options that can be applied to a group of cells in Excel. Each style includes a unique combination of number format, alignment, font, border style, pattern, and protection type. Cell styles can be a predefined style or a customized style to suit your requirements. These can also be locked to prevent others from editing them.

Example:

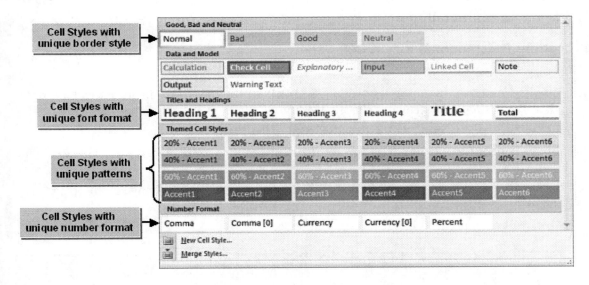

The Style Dialog Box

The Style dialog box contains various options that will allow you to modify an existing cell style and also create a new cell style. This dialog box can be accessed from the Cell Styles gallery in the Styles group on the Home tab. You can modify a cell style using the Modify option in the list that is displayed when you right-click the cell style in the gallery. You can create a new cell style using the New Cell Style option in the Cell Styles gallery. The modified and newly created cell style will be listed in the Cell Styles gallery.

The Style dialog box contains various options.

Style Dialog Box Option	Used To
Style Name text box	Specify the name of the style to be modified.
Format button	Display the Format Cells dialog box. The modifications to the formats used in the selected style can be made using this dialog box.
Style Includes section	Specify the formatting options to be included in the style. It contains the Number, Alignment, Font, Border Fill, and Protection check boxes that allow you to specify if these formatting options are to be included in the style or not.

How to Apply Cell Styles

Procedure Reference: Apply a Cell Style

To apply a cell style:

1. Select the range of cells to which you would like to apply the cell style.
2. On the Home tab, in the Styles group, click Cell Styles.
3. Select the desired cell style.

Procedure Reference: Modify a Cell Style

To modify a cell style:

1. On the Home tab, in the Styles group, click Cell Styles and in the displayed gallery, right-click the desired cell style and choose Modify to display the Style dialog box.
2. In the Style dialog box, click Format to display the Format Cells dialog box.
3. In the Format Cells dialog box, specify the modifications to be made to the cell style, and then click OK.
4. In the Style dialog box, in the Style Includes section, specify the changes to be made to the cell style.
5. Click OK to apply the changes to the cell style.

 When you apply a cell style to cells in the worksheet and modify it, the worksheet reflects the modified cell style automatically without applying the modified cell style again.

ACTIVITY 4-6
Applying Cell Styles

Before You Begin:
My New Calculations.xlsx is open.

Scenario:
You would like to format the cells in the worksheet so that it is visually apparent where values are to be input and where calculations will automatically update. You would also like to create a title style that can be used on all company worksheets.

What You Do	How You Do It
1. **Apply a cell style to the main heading.**	a. **Select cell A1.**
	b. On the Home tab, in the Styles group, **click Cell Styles** and in the displayed gallery, in the Titles And Headings section, **select Title.**

2. **Modify the font color of the applied cell style.**	a. In the Styles group, **click Cell Styles** and in the displayed gallery, in the Titles And Headings section, **right-click Title and choose Modify.**
	b. In the Style dialog box, **click Format** to display the Format Cells dialog box.
	c. In the Format Cells dialog box, **select the Font tab.**
	d. On the Font tab, **click the Color drop-down arrow** and in the displayed color gallery, in the Standard Colors section, **select a shade of blue.**
	e. **Click OK** to apply the changes and return to the Style dialog box.
	f. In the Style dialog box, **click OK** to modify the Title cell style.

3.	**Apply the Input style to the cells that contain data that is used in calculations.**	a.	**Select cells C8:F11 and cell H3.**
		b.	In the Styles group, **click Cell Styles** and in the Data And Model section, **choose Input.**

4.	**Apply the Calculation style to the cells that contain calculations.**	a.	**Select cells H8:L11, cells C13:F17, and cells C22:C27.**
		b.	In the Styles group, **click Cell Styles** and in the Data And Model section, **select Calculation.**
		c.	**Save and close the workbook.**

Lesson 4 Follow-up

In this lesson, you formatted a worksheet. Formatting worksheets improves their visual appeal, and it will visually differentiate one set of data from another, making it easier to quickly locate information.

1. **What type of formatting do you think that you would apply most often?**

2. **What types of formatting have you seen in worksheets where you felt there was inconsistent or excess formatting?**

5 | Printing Workbook Contents

Lesson Time: 50 minutes

Lesson Objectives:

In this lesson, you will print workbook contents.

You will:

- Print workbook contents using default print options.
- Set print options.
- Set page breaks.

Introduction

You have completed a workbook, and now you would now like to share the information stored in these files with other people. One way you can share the contents of your worksheets is by printing them. In this lesson, you will print the contents of a workbook.

You may be faced with situations where you are unable to share the contents of your worksheet electronically. Your computer may malfunction or your projection system may fail at an inopportune time in a meeting. Distributing printouts of your workbook enables you to continue with your work without hindrances. Excel provides options to prepare your workbook for producing printouts with effective layouts.

TOPIC A
Print Workbook Contents Using Default Print Options

In this lesson, you will print workbook contents. There are many ways to print, but the simplest is to use default options. In this topic, you will print workbook contents using default print options.

Assume that you have a long worksheet that contains data on sales associates and need to take a printout of data related to sales associates working in a particular city. To do so, you can define a range for this subset and take a printout of this range alone. Printing only a range of cells saves resources and also presents the reader with only the relevant information.

The Print Dialog Box

The Print dialog box provides options to set the various printing options before you print a worksheet.

Print Option	*Description*
Printer section	Options to find or select the printer. You can select or type the printer name in the Name text box.
Print Range section	Options to specify the range for printing. You can use these options to specify exactly which pages you want to print. If you need to print the entire workbook or worksheet, you can use the All option. To print selected pages, you can use the Page(s) option and specify the pages to be printed in the From and To spin boxes.
Print What section	Options to make specific selections for printing. You can print selected cells in the worksheet, active sheets, entire workbook, or just the tables in the workbook. You can also ignore or include particular portions on the worksheet that have been defined earlier. You can access these options using the Selection, Active Sheet, Entire Workbook, and Table options and the Ignore Print Areas check box.
Copies section	Option to specify the number of copies to be printed using the Number Of Copies text box and whether they are to be collated or not using the Collate check box.
Preview button	Enables you to view the preview of the print.
Properties button	Enables you to set the document properties.
Find Printer button	Enables you to find and add a printer.

The Print Area

If you need to frequently print a particular portion of a worksheet, you can set it is as a print area. Excel will print the print area by default. You can select the portion of the worksheet and use the Print Area drop-down menu to set the selected area as a print area, or clear a print area. You can also add another selection to the print area using the Add To Print Area option.

The Page Setup Dialog Box

The Page Setup dialog box contains various tabs with the different page setup options.

Tab	Description
Page	Contains options to set the page orientation, scaling percentage, paper size, print quality, and first page number.
Margins	Contains options for setting margins in worksheets.
Header/Footer	Contains options for setting the headers and footers for the worksheet.
Sheet	Contains options for setting print titles. You can also select the print area, set page order, and the print type.

Scaling Options

Excel provides scaling options in the Scale to Fit group on the Page Layout tab to enable you to restrict the printed output of a worksheet to a desired number of pages. You can scale to shrink the width or height to a desired number of pages, or you can shrink the worksheet to a specific percentage of the actual size. You can also use the Adjust To and Fit To options on the Page tab in the Page Setup dialog box to set the scaling for a worksheet.

Page Orientation

Definition:

Page orientation is a page layout setting that determines the position of content in a printed page. It specifies whether a page is to be printed vertically or horizontally. In Portrait orientation, the height of the page is greater than the width, and in Landscape orientation, width is greater than the height.

Example:

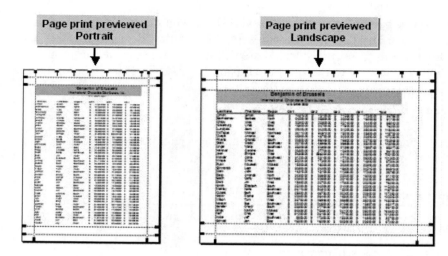

| Page print previewed Portrait | Page print previewed Landscape |

The Print Preview Option

You can use Print Preview to check how a worksheet or a workbook would appear in printed form, as well as to set the print options, change the page setup, or zoom and navigate through the preview.

Option	*Allows You To*
Print button	Print the desired worksheet(s) or the entire workbook.
Page Setup button	Change the page setup. Displays the Page Setup dialog box, which has options to change the page, margins, header and footer, and sheet settings.
Zoom button	Increase or decrease the magnification of the page preview.
Next Page button	Navigate to the next page.
Previous Page button	Navigate to the previous page.
Show Margins check box	View the header, footer, top, bottom, left, and right margins.
Close Print Preview button	Close print preview.

How to Print Workbook Contents

Procedure Reference: Preview the Workbook

To preview the workbook:

1. Click the Office button and choose Print→Print Preview, or press Ctrl+F2. (You can also open Print Preview from the Print and Page Setup dialog boxes.)

2. To magnify or reduce the page view, zoom in or zoom out using the Zoom button on the Ribbon, clicking the preview area of the document, or clicking the Zoom In or Zoom Out button on the Microsoft Office Status Bar.

3. To navigate through the previewed document, click the Next Page or Previous Page button in the Preview group on the Ribbon, or press Page Up or Page Down on the keyboard.

4. Click Close Print Preview or press Esc to return to the original document view.

Procedure Reference: Set or Clear the Print Area

To set or clear the print area:

1. In the worksheet, select the cells to set as the print area or select the cells that are currently set as the print area.

2. On the Page Layout tab, in the Page Setup group, click Print Area and choose Set Print Area or Clear Print Area.

3. If desired, to add additional ranges of cells, select the cells and choose Add To Print Area.

4. Save the workbook with the new print area settings.

Procedure Reference: Print an Excel Sheet

To print an Excel sheet:

1. If you want to print just a portion of the worksheet, select the range to print.

2. Click the Office button and choose Print. (You can also open the Print dialog box from the Page Setup dialog box or from Print Preview.)

3. If necessary, in the Print dialog box, in the Printer section, set the printer options.

4. In the Print Range section, select All to print all the pages, or select Page(s) and specify the page range in the From and To boxes.

5. In the Print What section, specify the components to be printed. You can print the current selection, the active sheets, the entire workbook, or only the table(s) in the worksheet.

6. By default, if you select Active Sheet(s) or Entire Workbook, Excel will print any set print area in the active sheet or workbook. To ignore the print area, check Ignore Print Areas.

7. In the Copies section, in the Number Of Copies spin box, specify the number of copies you want.

8. Check Collate to print multiple copies in collated order.

9. Click OK to print.

Procedure Reference: Change Page Orientation

To change page orientation:

1. Change the orientation of the worksheet.

    ●   In the Page Setup dialog box, on the Page tab, in the Orientation section, select Portrait to print vertically or Landscape to print horizontally.

    ●   Or, on the Page Layout tab, in the Page Setup group, click Orientation and select Portrait or Landscape.

2. Save the workbook to save the worksheet with the new orientation.

Procedure Reference: Scale the Range to be Printed

To scale the range to be printed:

1. Scale the printable range.

    ●   Scale the range using the Height, Width, or Scale options in the Scale To Fit group on the Page Layout tab.

    ●   Or, open the Page Setup dialog box and scale the range using the options in the Scaling section on the Page tab. You can adjust the scaling to a specific percentage, or fit the output to a specified number of pages wide by pages tall.

2. If desired, preview and print the workbook.

3. Save the workbook with the scaled settings.

ACTIVITY 5-1
Printing a Range of Selected Cells

Data Files:

Print.xlsx

Before You Begin:

A printer must be installed on your PC. From the C:\084890Data\Printing Workbook Contents folder, open the Print.xlsx file.

Scenario:

You're about to attend a meeting with your development team, and you have been asked to present the company's quarterly sales report in the meeting. However, they don't need all of the information; they only need to see the first 12 rows of the worksheet, so you want to set the first 12 rows in the worksheet as the default print area.

What You Do	How You Do It
1. Preview the print version of the Quarterly Sales Results worksheet.	a. Click the Office button and choose **Print→Print Preview**.
	b. On the Print Preview tab, in the Preview group, **click Next Page**. The Microsoft Office Status Bar indicates you are on page 2 of 2.
	c. In the Preview group, **click Close Print Preview**.
2. Preview the range of cells to be printed.	a. In the worksheet, **select cells A1:D12**.

	If you forget to select the range, or forget to choose Selection in the Print dialog box, then the entire worksheet will print.

	b. Click the Office button and choose Print.

c. In the Print dialog box, in the Print What section, **select the Selection option.**

d. **Click Preview** to preview the range of selected cells.

e. The selected range is displayed in Print Preview and there is only 1 page to be printed. **Close Print Preview.**

---

3. **Set the selected range of cells as the print area.**

a. With A1:D12 still selected, on the Page Layout tab, in the Page Setup group, **click Print Area and choose Set Print Area.**

b. **Click cell F1** to deselect the selected range of cells.

c. The marquee around the cells indicates the set print area. **Click the Office button and choose Print→Print Preview.**

d. Only the set print area displays in Print Preview. On the Print Preview tab, in the Print group, **click Print.**

e. In the Print dialog box, **click OK.**

f. **Save the workbook as *My Print.xlsx* and close it.**

ACTIVITY 5-2

Scaling and Orienting the Print Output

Data Files:

Books and Beyond.xlsx

Before You Begin:

From the C:\084890Data\Printing Workbook Contents folder, open the Books and Beyond.xlsx file.

Scenario:

The Books and Beyond report contains two pages of data. You would like to print the entire worksheet, horizontally, on a single page.

What You Do	How You Do It
1. **Preview the printed worksheet.**	a. **Click the Office button and choose Print→Print Preview.**
	b. **Examine the Microsoft Office Status Bar to see the number of pages to be printed.**
	c. **Press Page Down to see page 2 and then close Print Preview.**
2. **Scale the print version of the data in the worksheet.**	a. On the Page Layout tab, in the Page Setup group, **click Orientation and choose Landscape** to change the orientation of the worksheet.
	b. In the Scale To Fit group, **click the Width drop-down arrow and select 1 Page** to fit the width of the data in the worksheet into a single page.
3. **Preview the worksheet.**	a. **Click the Office button and choose Print→Print Preview.**
	b. The worksheet now fits on a single page. **Close the Print Preview.**
	c. **Save the file as *My Books and Beyond.xlsx* and then close the file.**

TOPIC B
Set Print Options

In the previous topic, you printed workbook contents using default print options. You can also adjust the print options to customize your output in various ways. In this topic, you will set print options.

It is difficult to read and interpret data that spans several pages of a single workbook. There are a number of print options you can set to improve the print output for large workbooks.

Workbook Views

You can display workbooks with different views using the Workbook Views group on the View tab.

Option	Allows You To
Normal	View the workbook in the Excel default view.
Page Layout View	View the workbook as it will appear in print along with the headers and footers.
Page Break Preview	Preview the workbook with page breaks that will be applied to the print output.
Custom Views	Create a custom view with a set of display and print settings.
Full Screen	View the workbook full screen without other screen elements.

Zoom Options

Excel allows worksheets to be zoomed in or out so that you can view the contents with the desired magnification. You can increase or decrease the magnification using the Zoom group on the View tab or the Zoom slider in the status bar. You can restore a document to its normal magnification using the 100% button in the Zoom group. You can use the Zoom To Selection option in the Zoom group to zoom to the selected cell or range of cells.

Print Titles

When a worksheet or workbook with multiple pages is printed, you can use the Print Titles command to print row and column titles on each page of a worksheet to make it easier to identify the contents of rows and columns. Row titles print at the top of each page, and column titles print at the left of each page. You can set up titles by using the Print Titles section of the Sheet tab in the Page Setup dialog box.

Headers and Footers

Definition:

A *header* or *footer* is a text or graphic block that repeats at the top or bottom of each printed page of your workbook. Excel headers and footers contain three sections: left, center, and right. The left text box on the left edge of the page, the center text box at the center, and the right text box on the right edge of the page. You can include any or all of the three sections in a header or footer. Each section can contain text or graphics that remain the same from page to page, or text that changes based on criteria, such as a page number or date.

Example:

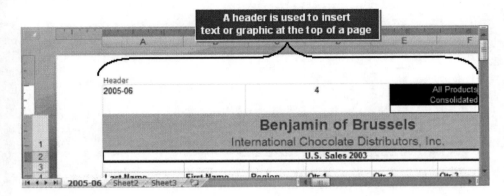

Header and Footer Settings

Excel provides you with options to create predefined or custom headers and footers. You can set the predefined header and footer for your workbook using the Header and Footer drop-down lists on the Header/Footer tab of the Page Setup dialog box, or the Header & Footer group on the Header & Footer Tools Design Contextual tab. You can use these settings to insert page numbers, page count, sheet number, predefined text, and so on. Alternatively, you can create custom headers and footers using the Custom Header and Custom Footer buttons on the Header/Footer tab of the Page Setup dialog box.

Page Margins

Definition:

A page *margin* is a boundary line that determines the amount of space between the worksheet data and the edge of the paper. Page margins define a region within which the contents of a page should fit. A page can have left, right, top, bottom, header, and footer margins. You can set predefined margins at Normal, Wide, and Narrow, or create custom margins.

Example:

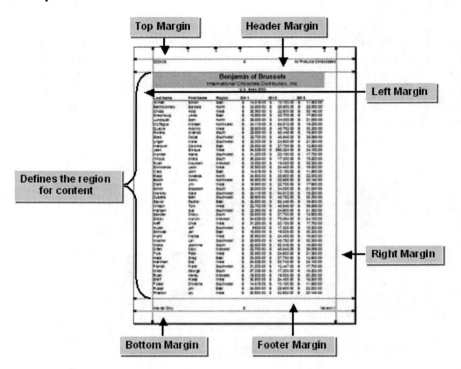

Margin Tab Options

The Margins tab of the Page Setup dialog box contains options to set values for the margins.

Option	Enables you to:
Left, Top, Header, Right, Bottom and Footer text boxes	Set the respective margin values using the Up or Down Arrow keys or by entering the value.
Center On Page section	Specify whether the content should be centered horizontally or vertically on the page.
Print button	Set print options by opening the Print dialog box.
Print Preview button	Preview the worksheet.
Options button	Allows you to set the document properties for the print output.

How to Set Print Options

Procedure Reference: Set or Remove a Print Title

To set or remove a print title:

1. Display the Page Setup dialog box.

    ● On the Page Layout tab, in the Page Setup group, click Print Titles.

    ● Or, on the Page Layout tab, in the Page Setup group, click the Dialog Box Launcher button.

2. On the Sheet tab, specify the print title or remove an existing print title.

    ● In the Print Titles section, click in the Rows To Repeat At Top text box or in the Columns To Repeat At Left text box. Select the rows or columns to use as the print title.

     You can click the Collapse Dialog button to the right of the text box to minimize the Page Setup dialog box and make it easier to select data in the worksheet. Press Enter or click the button again to expand the dialog box when you are done. Clicking anywhere in a row or column would select the entire row or column.

    ● To remove an existing print title, delete the print title set in the Rows To Repeat At Top and Columns To Repeat At Left text boxes.

3. In the Page Setup dialog box, click OK to apply the changes.

Procedure Reference: Create or Modify a Header or Footer Using the Page Setup Dialog Box

To create or modify a header or footer by using the Page Setup dialog box:

1. Display the Page Setup dialog box and select the Header/Footer tab.

2. To select a default header or footer, select it from the Header or Footer drop-down list.

3. If desired, to create or modify a custom header or footer, click Custom Header or Custom Footer and, in the Left Section, Center Section, or Right Section text boxes, enter data or insert data using the buttons in the Header or Footer dialog box.

4. Click OK to apply the header or footer settings to the worksheet.

Procedure Reference: Set Page Margins

To set page margins:

1. Display the Page Setup dialog box and select the Margins tab.

2. Adjust the top, left, right, bottom, header, and footer margin values by clicking the spin boxes or typing in the values.

     You can also set the page margins in the Print Preview window. In the Preview group, check the Show Margins check box to display the margin guides, then drag the margin guides until the desired margin value appears in the Microsoft Office Status Bar.

ACTIVITY 5-3
Setting Print Options

Data Files:

Report.xlsx

Before You Begin:

From the C:\084890Data\Printing Workbook Contents folder, open the Report.xlsx file.

Scenario:

You have been editing your sales report and, since you know it is too large to print on a single page, you want to adjust some print options to make the report's print output more attractive and readable.

● While previewing the document for printing purposes, you notice that only the first page of the worksheet displays the headings row and that the data is difficult to follow on the remaining pages.

● You want each page of the printout of the sales data worksheet to include the abbreviation of the company name, the sales region, the page number, and the number of pages in the report.

● You want to provide some additional white space at the bottom of the sales data in the sales report to be printed for distribution. You know that additional space at the bottom of the page will result in less data being displayed. You would like to reduce the space on either side of the sales data in the report to allow more data to be displayed.

What You Do	How You Do It
1. Preview the workbook.	a. Click the Office button and choose Print→Print Preview.
	b. Examine the preview and **close Print Preview**.
2. Set the print title.	a. On the Page Layout tab, in the Page Setup group, **click Print Titles**.

b. In the Page Setup dialog box, on the Sheet tab, in the Print Titles section, to the right of the Rows To Repeat At Top text box, **click the Collapse Dialog button.**

c. In the worksheet, **click anywhere in row 4** to set it as the print title to be repeated on every page of the printed worksheet.

d. In the Page Setup - Rows To Repeat At Top dialog box, **click the Collapse Dialog button** to expand the Page Setup dialog box.

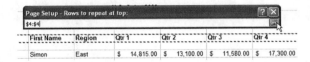

e. **Click OK** to apply the changes to the worksheet.

3. **Preview the print titles.**

   a. **Click the Office button and choose Print→Print Preview.**

   b. In the Print Preview window, **scroll down** to view the print titles on pages 2 and 3.

   c. **Close Print Preview.**

4. **Create the header.**

   a. In the Page Setup group, **click the Dialog Box Launcher button.**

   b. In the Page Setup dialog box, **select the Header/Footer tab.**

   c. **Click Custom Header** to display the Header dialog box.

   d. In the Left Section text box, **type *B of B***

   e. **Click in the Center Section text box and type *US Sales***

f. **Click in the Right Section text box and click the Insert Time button.**

g. **Click OK** to return to the Page Setup dialog box.

5. Create the footer.	a. In the Page Setup dialog box, from the Footer drop-down list, **select Page 1 Of ?.**
	b. **Click OK** to apply the header and footer to the worksheet.

6. Preview the header and footer.	a. **Click the Office button and choose Print→Print Preview.**
	b. On the Print Preview tab, in the Zoom group, **click Zoom** to increase the magnification and view the header.
	c. The left, center, and right headers appear at the top of the page. **Scroll down to view the footer.**

B of B   US Sales   4:28 PM

Benjamin of Brussels
International Chocolate Distributors, inc.

d. The page number appears in the footer. **Close Print Preview.**

Page 1 of 6

7. Set the bottom margin.	a. In the Page Setup group, **click the Dialog Box Launcher button.**
	b. In the Page Setup dialog box, **select the Margins tab.**

c. In the Bottom spin box, **click the up arrow twice** to scroll to the 1.5″ setting.

d. **Click Print Preview** to display the Print Preview window.

e. In the Print Preview window, in the Zoom group, **click Zoom** to fit the page within the viewable area of the screen.

f. In the Preview group, **check the Show Margins check box** to display the margin guides.

g. **Verify that the bottom margin is larger in size compared to the rest.**

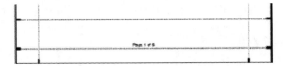

8. **Set the left and right margins.**

a. **Drag the left margin guide to the left until the reading at the left corner of the Microsoft Office Status Bar reads Left Margin: 0.25.**

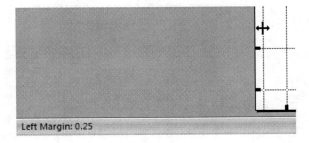

b. **Adjust the right margin to 0.25 inches.**

c. **Close Print Preview.**

d. **Save the workbook as *My Report.xlsx* and leave the file open for the next activity.**

TOPIC C
Set Page Breaks

You have changed the orientation of the worksheet to make the printed output more presentable. You would now like to specify where the data splits across the printed pages. In this topic, you will set page breaks.

A book is organized into lessons and chapters to present the contents in a logical order. Similarly, setting page breaks will help you ensure that related data is present on the appropriate pages. Adding page breaks to a worksheet prior to printing helps keep related information together on the printout.

Page Breaks

Definition:

Page breaks are lines that split the content across pages for print purposes. Page breaks are determined based on paper size, page orientation, number of pages, and any existing page breaks. Page breaks generated by the application are referred to as automatic page breaks, and those manually inserted are referred to as manual page breaks. An automatic page break is converted into a manual page break when you drag it.

Example:

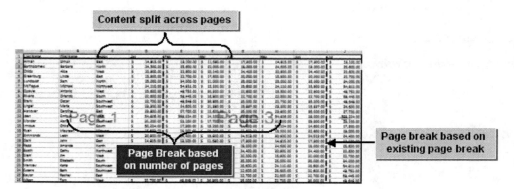

Page Break Options

You can insert manual page breaks using the options available in the Breaks drop-down menu of the Page Setup group.

Option	Description
Insert Page Break	Allows you to insert a manual page break above or to the left of the selected row or column.
Remove Page Break	Allows you to remove a manual page break above or to the left of the selected row or column.
Reset All Page Breaks	Removes all manual page breaks.

How to Set Page Breaks

Procedure Reference: Insert or Remove Page Breaks

To insert or remove page breaks:

1. Insert or remove page breaks.
   - Use the Page Layout tab to insert or remove page breaks.
     a. Select the row below or the column to the right of the page break location.
     b. On the Page Layout tab, in the Page Setup group, click Breaks and choose Insert Page Break or Remove Page Break. You can also choose Reset All Page Breaks to remove all manual page breaks.
   - Or, use the Page Break Preview window to insert or remove page breaks.
     a. To open the Page Break Preview window, click the Page Break Preview button near the Zoom slider or in the Workbook Views group on the View tab.
     b. Set or remove the page breaks.
        - In the Page Break Preview window, drag the automatic page break to the desired position, or drag it off the window to remove it.
        - In the worksheet, right-click a cell adjacent to the page break and choose Insert Page Break or Remove Page Break.
        - In the worksheet, select the desired row or column, right-click the selected row or column, and choose Insert Page Break or Remove Page Break.
        - Or, right-click any cell and choose Reset All Page Breaks to remove all manual page breaks.
     c. Return to Normal view.

 The benefit of Page Break Preview is that it shows the order in which the pages will print, not simply where the page breaks will occur.

ACTIVITY 5-4

Setting Page Breaks

Before You Begin:

My Report.xlsx is open.

Scenario:

The sales data worksheet that you are preparing for print has multiple pages. The pages are breaking in places that you don't want them to. For instance, the first page displays 17 rows of sales data. You want to check how the first page looks with 5 rows and then retain the best setting. Also, the last few columns of the sales data worksheet are not displayed on the first page to be printed, and you don't want the columns to be on a separate page.

What You Do	How You Do It
1. Preview the page to be printed with the default settings.	a. **Click the Office button and choose Print→Print Preview.**
	b. The first printed page contains 17 rows of sales data. **Close Print Preview.**
2. Insert a page break before row 15.	a. In the worksheet, **select row 15.**
	b. On the Page Layout tab, in the Page Setup group, **click Breaks and choose Insert Page Break.**
3. Preview the print version of the page.	a. **Click the Office button and choose Print→Print Preview.**
	b. Now the page has only 5 rows of data and there is a lot of blank space. **Close Print Preview.**

4.	**Preview the inserted page break in Page Break Preview.**	a.	On the Ribbon, **select the View tab.**
		b.	On the View tab, in the Workbook Views group, **click Page Break Preview.**
		c.	In the Welcome To Page Break Preview message box, **check the Do Not Show This Dialog Again check box and click OK.**
		d.	**Click cell A17** to view the inserted page break above row 15.
		e.	In the Workbook Views group, **click Normal.**

5.	**Delete the page break.**	a.	In the worksheet, **select row 15.**
		b.	On the Ribbon, **select the Page Layout tab.**
		c.	In the Page Setup group, **click Breaks and choose Remove Page Break.**
		d.	To verify that the page break has been deleted, **click cell A17** to deselect row 15.

14	Lundquist	Sam	North
15			
16	McTague	Michael	Northwest
17			
18	Quayle	Antonio	West

| 6. | **Move the automatic vertical page break.** | a. | On the View tab, in the Workbook Views groups, **click Page Break Preview.** |
| | | b. | There is an automatic page break to the right of column G, which will result in columns H, I, and J getting printed separately. **Drag the automatic page break after column G to the right, off the Page Break Preview.** |

c. The column page break is deleted and columns H, I, and J will print with the other columns. **Click Normal** to revert back to Normal view.

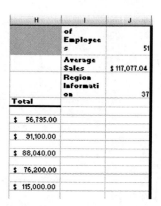

H	I	J
	of Employees	51
	Average Sales	$ 117,077.04
	Region Information	37
Total		
$ 56,795.00		
$ 91,100.00		
$ 88,040.00		
$ 76,200.00		
$ 115,000.00		

d. **Examine the scale percentage on the Page Layout tab in the Scale To Fit group.**

7. **Preview the page.**

a. **Click the Office button and choose Print→Print Preview.**

b. The page should display 17 rows of the sales data and the data in the top-right corner of the worksheet should appear in full. **Close Print Preview.**

c. **Save and close the workbook.**

Lesson 5 Follow-up

In this lesson, you printed the contents of a workbook. Printing allows you to distribute your workbooks when it's not feasible to distribute them electronically.

1. **How will you set up the headers and footers in your workbooks? Please give some examples.**

2. **What are some reasons you might need to print column or row headings for your work?**

6 Managing Large Workbooks

Lesson Time: 1 hour(s)

Lesson Objectives:

In this lesson, you will manage large workbooks.

You will:

- Format worksheet tabs.
- Manage worksheets in a workbook.
- Manage the view of large worksheets.

Introduction

Throughout this course, you've been building worksheets that are more and more complex. As worksheets get larger and contain more data, there are specific techniques you can use to manage, view, and navigate within the workbook. In this lesson, you will manage large workbooks.

There are many unique issues that come into play in larger workbooks. You might have more sheets that contain data. You might have individual sheets you need to rearrange. You might have to compare or work with content that is located in distant areas of the workbook. With the proper tools and skills, you can manage large workbooks so that you can access and view specific areas of the worksheet efficiently.

TOPIC A
Format Worksheet Tabs

In this lesson, you will manage large workbooks. One way to manage multiple tabs in large workbooks is to customize their formatting. In this topic, you will format worksheet tabs.

Imagine a file cabinet with multiple file folders that are all the same color. It might be difficult to find information if everything looks the same. However, if the folders had a color coding system that indicated the type of content that is in a particular folder, then it would be easier to visually scan the folders and quickly access the data you need. Formatting worksheet tabs in an Excel workbook is much like color-coding traditional file folders. It helps you organize and quickly locate the information you need.

Tab Formatting Options

Excel allows you to rename and change the color of worksheet tabs. You can change the sheet names to something more meaningful, so that you can quickly locate the appropriate data. Changing the color of a tab can be another way to distinguish the type of data that resides on a sheet.

How to Format Worksheet Tabs
Procedure Reference: Format Worksheet Tabs

To change the name or color of a worksheet tab:
1. On the sheet tab bar, select the desired worksheet tab's default name.
    *   Right-click the Worksheet tab and choose Rename.
    *   Or, double-click the worksheet tab.
2. Type the new name for the worksheet and then press Enter.
3. Color the worksheet tab.
    *   Right-click the worksheet tab(s) you want to color, choose Tab Color, and then select a desired color.
    *   Or, on the Home tab, in the Cells group, click Format, choose Tab Color, and then select the color of your choice.

ACTIVITY 6-1
Formatting Worksheet Tabs

Data Files:

Divisions.xlsx

Before You Begin:

From the C:\084890Data\Managing Large Workbooks folder, open the Divisions.xlsx file.

Scenario:

The workbook that stores data for the divisions is organized on multiple worksheets. The workbook consists of two regional worksheets and a separate summary worksheet. Identifying the worksheets becomes difficult because each sheet is named with a default generic sheet number instead of descriptive labels. You would like to rename the worksheets and color code the sheet tabs to more easily distinguish them.

What You Do	How You Do It
1. Examine the three worksheets in this workbook.	a. Verify that the Sheet1 tab contains data specific to the Australian division.
	b. Click the Sheet2 tab and verify this sheet has data specific to the European Division.
	c. Click Sheet3 and verify it contains a summary for both divisions.
2. Rename the first worksheet as *Australian*.	a. On the sheet tab bar, **right-click the Sheet1 worksheet tab and choose Rename.**
	b. **Type *Australian* and press Enter** to rename the tab.
	Australian / Sheet2
3. Rename the second and third worksheets as *European* and *Summary*, respectively.	a. **Double-click the Sheet2 worksheet tab** to select its default name.
	b. **Type *European* and press Enter.**

c. Rename the third worksheet as *Summary*

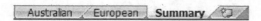

4. Change the color of the tabs.

a. **Right-click the Summary worksheet tab and choose Tab Color.**

b. In the Tab Color gallery, in the Standard Colors section, **select Yellow.**

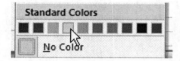

c. **Change the tab colors of the Australian and European sheets to suit your preference.**

d. **Save the workbook as *My Divisions* and leave the file open for the next activity.**

TOPIC B

Manage Worksheets in a Workbook

Throughout this lesson, you are managing large worksheets. A good management technique is to control the positioning and appearance of the sheets within a workbook. In this topic, you will manage worksheets in a workbook.

There may be times where you have entered data into different worksheets based on when you received the data, or based on the type of data contained in the worksheet, but after time you may realize that the sheets are not in a logical order or some of the worksheets may no longer be necessary. You can easily reposition worksheets in Excel or delete them if they are no longer necessary.

Methods of Repositioning Worksheets

Excel gives you several tools you can use to move or copy worksheets within the same workbook or between workbooks. You can reposition worksheets by using the Move Or Copy dialog box, by opening the shortcut menu for a worksheet, or by manually dragging and dropping a worksheet to its new location.

Methods of Inserting or Deleting Worksheets

To insert new worksheets, you can use the Insert Worksheet tab next to the last sheet, or the Insert Sheet option in the Insert menu of the Cells group. You can also insert a worksheet by using the Insert dialog box. Right-click the worksheet tab and choose Insert from the shortcut menu to open the dialog box. Use the dialog box to insert a blank worksheet, or a worksheet based on a local template or a template from Office Online.

To delete worksheets with unwanted or obsolete data, you can use the Delete Sheet option in the Delete drop-down list of the Cells group, or choose delete from a worksheet tab's shortcut menu.

The Hide and Unhide Worksheet Options

When you have multiple worksheets open, you may need to hide sheets that are not currently required so that your workspace is not cluttered. You can hide a selected worksheet by using the Hide Sheet option on the Hide & Unhide submenu of the Format menu in the Cells group. You can also hide a sheet using the Hide option in the shortcut menu that is displayed when you right-click the worksheet tab.

When you need to unhide a worksheet, choose Unhide Sheet from the Hide & Unhide submenu to open the Unhide dialog box and reveal the names of the hidden sheets. You can also choose Unhide from the shortcut menu of the worksheet tab.

Worksheet References in Formulas

You can create formulas that contain references to cells or ranges that are on other sheets of the workbook. You can type references or enter them by clicking on the sheet and cells to which you want to refer. For example, the following formula adds the contents of all cells A2 in Sheet 2, Sheet 3, Sheet 4, and Sheet 5: =SUM(Sheet2:Sheet5!A2)

How to Manage Worksheets in a Workbook

Procedure Reference: Move or Copy Worksheets

To move or copy worksheets within or between workbooks:

1. Right-click the worksheet tab and choose Move Or Copy to display the Move Or Copy dialog box.

2. From the Move Selected Sheets To Book drop-down list, select the destination workbook. You can move or copy to the existing workbook, another open workbook, or to a new workbook.

3. In the Before Sheet list box, select the worksheet before which the selected worksheet(s) need(s) to be moved or copied.

4. If you want to copy the sheet rather than move it, check the Create A Copy check box.

5. Click OK.

 To manually move sheets within a workbook, on the sheet tab bar, drag the worksheet tab to the new position.

Procedure Reference: Insert or Delete Worksheets

To insert or delete a worksheet:

1. Insert or delete a worksheet.
    - Insert new sheets.
        - Right-click the worksheet tab to the left of which the new worksheet needs to be added, choose Insert, verify that the Worksheet option is selected, and click OK;
        - Or, on the sheet tab bar, to the right of the worksheet tabs, click the Insert Worksheet button to insert the new worksheet.
    - Right-click the worksheet(s) and choose Delete to delete sheets.

Procedure Reference: Hide or Unhide Worksheets

To hide or unhide worksheets:

1. Hide or unhide worksheets.
    - Select the worksheet(s) you want to hide, right-click the selected tab(s), and then choose Hide to hide the worksheet(s).
    - Unhide sheets.
        a. Right-click any worksheet tab on the sheet tab bar, and then choose Unhide.
        b. In the Unhide dialog box, in the Unhide Sheet list box, select the hidden worksheet you want to display and click OK.

ACTIVITY 6-2
Managing Worksheets

Before You Begin:
My Divisions.xlsx is open.

Scenario:
The expenditure incurred by each division is tracked on an individual worksheet in an Excel workbook, and you would like to organize these worksheets based on your information needs and changes in your company's organization.

● You want the Summary sheet first.

● You need a new sheet for the new North American division that will have similar contents to the Australian Division.

● You need a brand-new sheet for all employees.

● Finally, you would like to use this workbook at a presentation. You don't want all the divisions to be seen for the presentation.

What You Do	How You Do It
1. **Examine the formulas on the Summary worksheet.**	a. On the Summary worksheet, **select B4.** b. **Examine the formula in the formula box.**
2. **Move the Summary worksheet to the first sheet position in the workbook.**	a. Using your mouse, **press and hold the Summary tab until a small arrow is displayed near the top-left corner of the tab and the pointer changes to a page icon pointer.**  b. **Drag the worksheet until the arrow points to the left of the Australian tab.**

3. **Copy the Australian worksheet.**

    a. **Right-click the Australian tab and choose Move Or Copy.**

    b. In the Before Sheet list box, **verify that the destination is the current workbook and select European.**

    c. **Check the Create A Copy check box.**

    d. **Click OK.**

4. **Enter data into the North American Division worksheet.**

    a. In cell A1, **type *N American Division***

    b. **Rename the new worksheet *N American* and give the tab a new color.**

    c. **Clear cells B4:E7.**

    d. In the N American worksheet, in cell B4, **type *500* and press Enter.**

    e. On the Summary worksheet, **select and examine cell B4.**

5. **Add a new worksheet to the workbook that will contain an employee listing for all the divisions.**

    a. **Right-click the European tab and choose Insert.**

    b. **Verify that Worksheet is selected and click OK.**

    c. **Move the new worksheet to the end of the workbook.**

    d. **Rename the new worksheet *Employees* and give the tab the color of your choice.**

6. **Hide all sheets except the Summary worksheet.**

   a. **Right-click the Employees tab and choose Hide.**

   b. **Click the Australian tab and Shift-click the European tab.**

   c. **Right-click any of the selected tabs and choose Hide.**

   d. **Verify that Summary is the only worksheet visible and the formulas are still accurate.**

7. **Unhide the European and Australian worksheets.**

   a. **Right-click the Summary tab and choose Unhide.**

   b. In the Unhide Sheet list box, **select European.**

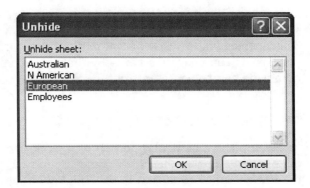

   c. **Click OK** to display the worksheet.

   d. **Unhide the Australian worksheet.**

   e. **Save the workbook and leave the file open for the next activity.**

TOPIC C
Manage the View of Large Worksheets

In the previous topic, you managed worksheets within a workbook. Once worksheets are arranged to your liking, you might need to control the overall view of the worksheet. In this topic, you will manage the view of large worksheets.

If you have worked with a report with many pages, you probably remember that as you made changes it was hard to keep track of what information was on a particular page, or if new information that was added would remain on the same page. You may have had to refer back to column headings that were on a previous page to know if you were looking at the correct column. In Excel, you can make sure that the column or row headings are always available, and that you know, before you print, what information will appear on the page.

The Split Option

When you work with large worksheets, you may need to view different portions of the sheet simultaneously. You can split a worksheet into multiple resizable panes using the Split option. This enables you to view distant parts of the worksheet by scrolling through the different panes. You can resize the panes by dragging the split bars that separate the panes. The Split command can be accessed from the Window group of the View tab.

Freeze Panes Options

You can make a particular portion of a worksheet remain static while you scroll through the other areas by using the Freeze Panes options. You can access the Freeze Panes options from the Freeze Panes command in the Window group on the View tab. When you select one of these options, it acts as a toggle, and the Unfreeze Panes option is displayed in place of Freeze Panes. This allows you to unfreeze rows, columns, and panes.

You can make portions of a worksheet static using the Freeze Panes options.

Option	Description
Freeze Panes	Allows you to keep the portion of the worksheet above the selected row and column static while you scroll through the other rows and columns.
Freeze Top Row	Allows you to keep the top row static while scrolling through the other portions of the worksheet.
Freeze First Column	Allows you to keep the first column static while scrolling through the other portions of the worksheet.

The Arrange Windows Dialog Box

The Arrange command, in the Window group on the View tab, displays the Arrange Windows dialog box. The Arrange Windows dialog box contains options to specify the arrangement of windows in the Excel interface. You can arrange the windows in a tiled, horizontal, vertical, or cascade manner. The Windows Of Active Workbook check box can be used to display only the windows of the current workbook.

The Arrange Windows dialog box provides options to arrange windows in different ways.

Option	Description
Tiled	You can view all the open windows as rectangles covering the entire workbook window.
Horizontal	You can view all the open windows, one below the other.
Vertical	You can view all the windows that are open, one next to the other.
Cascade	You can view all the open windows displayed one behind the other.

How to Manage the View of Large Worksheets

Procedure Reference: Split a Worksheet Window

To split a worksheet window:

1. Select the cell in the worksheet where you want to split the screen
2. On the Ribbon, on the View tab, in the Window group, click Split.
3. When finished with the split, remove it.
   - On the View tab, in the Window group, click Split.

Procedure Reference: Freeze or Unfreeze Panes

To freeze or unfreeze panes:

1. Freeze or unfreeze panes.
   - To freeze only the first row or column, on the View tab, in the Window group, click Freeze Panes and select Freeze Top Row or Freeze First Column.
   - To freeze both rows and columns, on the View tab, in the Window group, click Freeze Panes and select Freeze Panes.
   - To unfreeze the panes, on the View tab, in the Window group, click Freeze Panes and select Unfreeze Panes.

Procedure Reference: Arrange Worksheets within a Workbook in Separate Windows

To arrange worksheets within a workbook so you can see them in separate windows:

1. With the workbook open, on the View tab, in the Window group, click New Window to open the entire workbook in a new window.
2. Repeat step 1 until you have a new window for every worksheet you want to view in the workbook.
3. In the Window group, click Arrange All to display the Arrange Windows dialog box and select the desired display option.

4. If you have multiple workbooks open, check the Windows Of Active Workbook check box so that you don't arrange windows of other open workbooks.

5. Click OK.

ACTIVITY 6-3
Managing the View of a Large Worksheet

Data Files:

Sales.xlsx

Before You Begin:

My Divisions.xlsx is open. From the C:\084890Data\Managing Large Workbooks folder, open the Sales.xlsx file.

Scenario:

You are reviewing data in a sales report. Due to the large amount of data in the sheet, it's getting difficult to keep your focus on the specific data. You want to read the contents of the Total column and confirm that the column contains the correct data for each employee. For better readability, you want to see the Name columns next to the Total column.

You want to compare some of the values in the European Division, Australian Division, and Summary worksheets of the My Divisions workbook. You need to be able to view the contents of all three worksheets simultaneously.

What You Do	How You Do It
1. Split the Sales worksheet window.	a. In the Sales.xlsx worksheet, **scroll through the worksheet to see its data.**
	b. **Select cell C5.**
	c. On the Ribbon, **select the View tab.**
	d. On the View tab, in the Window group, **click Split.** [⊞ Split]
	e. **Verify that the vertical and horizontal split bars appear.**

Last Name	First Name	Region	Qtr 1	Qtr 2
Arman	Simon	East	$ 14,815.00	$ 13,100.00
Bartholomew	Barbara		$ 24,500.00	$ 25,600.00

2.	**Freeze the panes.**	a.	In the Window group, **click Freeze Panes and select Freeze Panes.**
		b.	In the worksheet, **scroll down and verify that the column headings remain visible.**
		c.	In the worksheet, **scroll to the right and verify that the Total column can be displayed next to the employee names.**
3.	**Unfreeze the panes.**	a.	In the Window group, **click Split** to remove the split bars.
		b.	**Scroll through the worksheet to verify the panes are gone.**
		c.	**Close the Sales workbook without saving it.**
4.	**Create two new windows to view the My Divisions worksheet.**	a.	With My Divisions.xlsx open, in the Window group, **click New Window** to create a new window. ▣ New Window
		b.	The My Divisions workbook opens in a new window with the title My Divisions.xlsx:2 - Microsoft Excel. **Create one more new window.**
5.	**Tile the windows and arrange the worksheets.**	a.	In the Window group, **click Arrange All** to display the Arrange Windows dialog box.
		b.	In the Arrange Windows dialog box, **verify that the Tiled option is selected and click OK.**

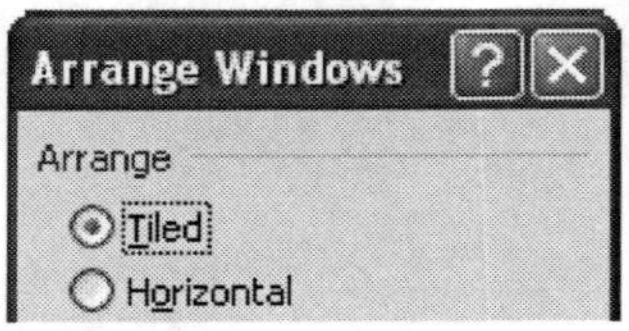

6. **Display a different worksheet in each of the windows.**

a. **Select a window and click the Summary worksheet tab.**

b. **Select each of the other windows and display the European tab in one and the Australian tab in the other.**

c. **Save and close the workbook.**

d. **Click the Office button, and then click Exit Excel.**

Lesson 6 Follow-up

In this lesson, you managed large workbooks. These techniques will enable you to access and view specific areas of the worksheet efficiently.

1. **Why might you want to customize the layout of your Excel workspace?**

2. **What other ways would you like to customize the layout of your workbooks in Excel?**

Follow-up

In this course, you used Excel to manage, edit, and print data. Storing data electronically is more efficient than storing it in a paper-based system because it allows you to quickly update existing data, run reports on the data, calculate totals, and chart, sort, and filter your data.

1. **What data are you currently working with that would be better stored in Excel? How might you begin the migration process from paper to electronic storage?**

2. **Consider your current work environment. What projects do you think would become more efficient if Excel was used either as an element of the project or if the entire project was controlled and manipulated within Excel?**

3. **Consider your current work environment. What data are you working with now that could benefit from being sorted, charted, or filtered to help make business decisions?**

What's Next?

The *Microsoft Office Excel 2007: Level 1* course helped you understand the basics of Excel and prepared you to go to the Element K course, *Microsoft Office Excel 2007: Level 2*.

Lesson Labs

Due to classroom setup constraints, some labs cannot be keyed in sequence immediately following their associated lesson. Your instructor will tell you whether your labs can be practiced immediately following the lesson or whether they require separate setup from the main lesson content.

Lesson 1 Lab 1

Creating a Basic Worksheet

Before You Begin:

Launch the Microsoft Office Excel 2007 application.

Scenario:

You are the sales manager of a company. In an Excel spreadsheet, you want to document the sales people's monthly totals for the first quarter. You have recorded the January sales as 410, 385, and 520 for Miller, Doyle, and Johnson, respectively. The February sales are 390, 405, and 500, respectively, and the March sales are 470, 440, and 540, respectively. You will include a Totals column which you will calculate at a later time. Also, you want to send this file for others to use, so you will save the spreadsheet in the current file format and then save it in an earlier format because they may still have Excel 2003 on their systems.

---

1. **Create a new Excel workbook.**

---

2. In the worksheet, in cells B2, C2, D2, E2, and F2, **enter the column headings as *Name, Jan, Feb, Mar,* and *Totals*** respectively, to create five new column headings.

---

3. In the Name column, **enter the labels *Miller, Doyle,* and *Johnson* in cells B3, B4, and B5, respectively.**

---

4. In the Jan column, **enter the January sales for the respective sales people.**

---

5. In the Feb column, **enter the February sales for the respective sales people.**

---

6. In the Mar column, **enter the March sales for the respective sales people.**

---

7. **Perform a compatibility check on the worksheet.**

---

8. **Save the workbook in the current file format and also make a copy in an earlier file format.**

Lesson 2 Lab 1

Executing Formulas and Functions

Data Files:

Tierone Calculations.xlsx

Before You Begin:

Open the Tierone Calculations.xlsx file from the C:\084890Data\Performing Calculations folder.

Scenario:

You are the accounts executive of your company and have received the company's financial worksheet. The sales income for each product and the sales tax rate have been specified in the worksheet. The amount of the total company expenses has also been specified in the worksheet. You need to calculate the company's total income, net income, taxes, and profit after tax.

---

1. Use a function to calculate the total income.

---

2. Calculate the net income by deducting the expenses from the total income.

---

3. Calculate the taxes by multiplying the net income with the tax rate constant value.

---

4. Calculate the profit after taxes by deducting the tax value from the net income value.

---

5. Save the workbook.

Lesson 3 Lab 1

Reorganizing a Worksheet

Data Files:

Tierone Baskets.xlsx

Before You Begin:

Open the Tierone Baskets.xlsx file from the C:\084890Data\Modifying a Worksheet folder.

Scenario:

You are the sales executive of the Gourmet Gifts To Go company. You have tracked the company's projected sales values for half of the year on an Excel worksheet, and you would like to modify the worksheet before sending it to your manager. You notice that the cost price value should appear next to the relevant label. You want to create additional columns for the months February through June and fill in the sales values. You've forgotten to include two other gift items, Fruit and Chocolate, and their prices, which should be arranged in Tier 1. You would like to change the specialty item to a more detailed name. You also realize that you have given a wrong subtitle in the spreadsheet. Finally, you decide to spell check the entire spreadsheet and save a copy of the workbook with changes before sending it to your manager.

1. **Move the cost price value in cell D13 to the respective row.**

2. After January, **add columns for the months February through June and enter their sales values as 100, 85, 150, 175, and 210, respectively.**

3. Below the existing row 10, **insert two rows** to include to more gift items.

4. In addition to Specialty and Cheese, **include the items *Fruit* and *Chocolate* with their tier values, respectively.**

5. In the Price column, **include the prices for the gifts, Fruit and Chocolate, as *27* and *32* (in dollars), respectively.**

6. **Edit cell A8 so that it reads *Specialty Coffee.***

7. **Replace the word "protected" with "projected."**

8. **Spell check the worksheet and correct the misspelled words.**

9. **Save the file.**

Lesson 4 Lab 1

Enhancing a Worksheet

Data Files:

Sales Revenue.xlsx

Before You Begin:

Open the Sales Revenue.xlsx file from the C:\084890Data\Formatting a Worksheet folder.

Scenario:

You have recorded the sales revenue generated by each employee in your division. You would like to distinguish the column headings and Totals rows from the rest of the worksheet. The title of the worksheet should also be distinguishable. The values need to be displayed as sales figures. The employee numbers need to be formatted to conform to company standards. While enhancing the worksheet, you will use the following specifications set by your company:

- The font type, size, and style of the column headings should be Arial, 10 pt, Bold.
- Column headings should be centered.
- The Top And Thick Bottom border should be used to distinguish the column headings and Totals rows from other information in the worksheet.
- Employee numbers are formatted using "ID"-##-####.
- The cell style of choice is 40% – Accent 1.
- All values representing dollars and cents should be formatted using the Accounting format so that decimal points and dollar signs are always aligned.

1. Modify the font type, size, and style of the column headings, and align them to meet company specifications.

2. Add a border to the column headings and Totals rows.

3. Modify the background cell color of the column headings and Totals rows to a color that you desire.

4. Create a custom number format according to your company's specifications—*"ID"-##-####.*

5. Apply the company standard cell style to the employee IDs and names.

6. Merge and center the contents of cell A1 across the range A1:C2.

7. **Apply the cell style Heading 1 to the title of the worksheet.**

8. **Apply the Accounting number format to E6:P6 and E20:P20, choosing 2 decimal places and $ as the symbol.**

9. **Apply the Accounting number format to E7:P16, choosing 2 decimal places and None as the symbol.**

10. **Save the file.**

Lesson 5 Lab 1

Creating a Printout of a Workbook

Data Files:

Lone Pine.xlsx

Before You Begin:

Open the Lone Pine.xlsx file from the C:\084890Data\Printing Workbook Contents folder.

Scenario:

You are preparing the Lone Pine workbook for hard-copy distribution at a meeting. You want to see the entire width of the workbook on a single page. The first five rows of the workbook should appear on each page of the printout. You also want Page X of Y to appear at the bottom of every page, where X equals the current page and Y equals the total number of pages in the printed document. The first page should contain the July data, the second page should have all the August data, and the third page should have all the September data.

1. **Preview or print the workbook.**

2. **Change the page orientation to Landscape.**

3. **Set rows 1 through 5 as the print title.**

4. **Add a footer that identifies the current page and the total pages of the printed document (Page X of Y).**

5. **Add page breaks between the monthly data as required.**

6. **Save the workbook.**

7. **Preview or print the workbook.**

Lesson 6 Lab 1

Managing Large Workbooks

Data Files:

Company Info.xlsx

Before You Begin:

Open the Company Info.xlsx file from the C:\084890Data\Managing Large Workbooks.

Scenario:

You have consolidated your company information into a single workbook. The workbook contains six worksheets, and you decide to apply some formatting to the worksheet tabs. There are also blank worksheets that you want deleted. You would like to organize the worksheets in a particular order, and you want to create a new workbook out of the payroll information provided in one of the worksheets. In the new workbook created from the payroll information provided, you want to freeze the column headings of the Payroll Info worksheet on the screen so that you will always see them as you scroll through the worksheet.

1. **Delete Sheet3 and Sheet5.**

2. **Name the worksheets, starting from the left, as *Programmers, Payroll Info, Holidays,* and *Schedule.***

3. **Reposition the worksheet tabs in the following order: Payroll Info, Programmers, Schedule, and Holidays.**

4. **Color the worksheet tabs.**

5. **Create a new workbook from the payroll information provided in the Payroll Info worksheet.**

6. In the new workbook, **freeze the column headings on the Payroll Info worksheet.**

7. **Save the new workbook and the original workbook.**

Solutions

Glossary

absolute reference
A cell reference in a formula that does not change when you copy the formula.

active cell
The cell that is selected in any worksheet is the active cell.

application window
The outer window of Excel, which usually fills the entire screen and provides an interface for you to interact with Excel.

arguments
The data provided to the function to run calculations.

Auto Fill feature
Fills a selected range of cells with selected data. This is done by entering data into one or more cells and dragging the fill handle to the other cells.

cell style
A collection of individual format options that you can apply to selected cells.

contextual tabs
A command tab that appears on the Ribbon only when you select specific objects on the worksheet such as a chart, table, drawing, text box, or WordArt.

contiguous range
Cells that are adjacent to each other.

Excel 2007
An application in the Microsoft Office suite that can be used to create, revise, and save data in a spreadsheet format.

Excel formula
A set of mathematical instructions that can be used to perform calculations in Excel worksheets.

Excel Help window
A window that provides a quick and easy way to find answers to questions related to Excel.

fill handle
The box at the corner of a cell or range that you can use to activate the Excel Auto Fill feature.

font
A predefined typeface that can be used for formatting characters.

footer
A text or graphic block that prints at the bottom of each page.

Formula AutoComplete
A dynamic feature in Excel that allows you to conveniently choose and enter formulas and functions.

Formula Bar
An interface component of Excel 2007 that contains the Name Box, the Insert Function button, and the formula box for specifying formulas.

Function Library
A large command group on the Formulas tab that holds several categories of functions.

function name
An abbreviated name of a function.

function
A built-in formula in Excel.

gallery
A repository for elements of the same category that acts as a central location for accessing the various styles and appearance settings for any one object.

header
A text or graphic block that prints at the top of each page.

Live Preview
A dynamic feature that allows you to preview how formatting options will look on a worksheet before you actually apply the selected formatting.

margin
A margin determines the amount of space between the worksheet data and the edge of the paper.

Microsoft Office Status Bar
An interface component that is located at the bottom of the application window and contains improvised features.

mixed reference
A cell reference in a formula that contains both an absolute and a relative reference.

noncontiguous range
Cells that are not adjacent to each other.

number format
A number format is a data format that changes the appearance of the numerical data in a cell.

Office button
A standard button located at the top-left corner of the Excel window that contains commands to open, save, send, print, close, finish, and publish worksheets.

page breaks
Are lines that split the content across pages for print purposes.

Page orientation
The arrangement of content in a page.

Quick Access toolbar
A customizable toolbar that provides easy access to frequently used commands in the application.

relative reference
A cell reference in a formula that changes when a formula is copied from one position to another, to reflect the new position.

Ribbon
A unique interface component that contains task-specific commands that are grouped together under different command tabs.

spreadsheet
A paper or electronic document that stores various types of data, such as numbers, text, and non-alphanumeric symbols, in a tabular format.

template
A template is a pre-designed workbook with pre-configured formatting, formulas, and text. It does not contain actual data.

typeface
The style or design of a set of characters.

workbook window
The inner window of Excel, which appears within the application window and displays a workbook in which to enter and store data.

workbook
A repository of related worksheets.

worksheet
An Excel worksheet is an electronic spreadsheet.

Index

A

absolute reference, 45
  creating, 47
active cell, 4
Alignment options, 92
application window, 3
arguments, 35
Auto Fill feature, 54
Auto Fill options, 55
AutoComplete feature
  applying a formula, 37
AutoFill
  filling cells with a series of data, 56

B

Border options, 77
borders
  adding to cells, 78
  removing from cells, 79

C

cell data
  aligning, 93
  editing, 56
  finding, 63
  going to, 63
  wrapping contents, 94
Cell Merge options, 92
cell names, 63
cell style, 97
  applying, 98
  modifying, 98
cells
  merging, 93
  naming, 63

columns, 4
  changing width by dragging boundaries, 83
  hide, 83
Compatibility Checker, 21
contextual tabs, 7
Copy Cells option, 55
Copy option, 44
Cut option, 44

D

data
  moving between cells, 56

E

Error Checking button, 36
Excel 2007, 3
Excel formula
  elements, 31
Excel formulas, 30
Excel Help window, 16
  areas of search, 16

F

file types, 21
fill handle, 54
Find command, 62
  advanced options, 62
fonts, 72
Fonts, 72
  changing type, 74
footer
  settings, 113
Format Cells dialog box, 72
formula
  applying using AutoComplete feature, 37

S

Save As dialog box, 20
ScreenTips, 8
Search Button
  obtaining help, 17
Selection options, 13
sheet background
  adding color, 78
Sheet Background, 77
Spelling dialog box, 66
spreadsheet, 2
Style dialog box, 97

T

tab formatting options, 128
Table of Contents pane, 17
template, 20
Transpose option, 82
typeface, 72

U

Undo options, 54
Unhide commands
  columns, 82
  rows

W

workbook, 4

creating a new workbook, 22
  previewing, 107
  saving, 22
  saving changes, 22
workbook views, 112
workbook window, 3
worksheet, 4
  spell checking, 67
worksheet tabs
  changing the color, 128
worksheets
  changing the name, 128
  inserting, 131, 132
  methods of repositioning, 131
  printing, 107
  repositioning by using Move or Copy dialog box,
    132
Wrap Text option, 93

X

XML, 21
  Also See: Word 2007 file types

Z

Zoom options, 112

Looking for media files?

They are now conveniently located at www.elementk.com/courseware-file-downloads

Downloading is quick and easy:

1. Visit www.elementk.com/courseware-file-downloads
2. In the search field, type in either the part number or the title
3. Of the courseware titles displayed, choose your title by clicking on the name
4. Links to the data files are located in the middle of the screen
5. Follow the instructions on the screen based upon your web browser

Note that there may be other files available for download in addition to the course files.

Approximate download times:

The amount of time it takes to download your data files will vary according to the file's size and your Internet connection speed. A broadband connection is highly recommended. The average time to download a 10 mb file on a broadband connection is less than 1 minute.